Echoes Of An Ancient Word

*"The Power of Apostolic Christianity Brought to
Life in the Stories of Our Own Day and Time..."*

BOOK I
in the
Trinity Collection

by Doug Michaud

*For I decided to know nothing among you
except Jesus Christ and Him crucified...
and my speech and my message were not in
plausible words of wisdom, but in demonstration
of the Spirit and of power, that your faith might
not rest in the wisdom of men but in the power of God...*
— Paul of Tarsus

To Paul,
my first brother, my first friend and best man...

Author's Note

There are key scriptual citations provided in the Index as study notes accompanying the text. These biblical references are not proof texts. They are provided only to show the motive and origin of my thought in the light of scripture. They can then serve to stimulate your further reflection and prayer, perhaps most effectively after a first reading of the book.

Doug Michaud
Long Island
Christmas Night
1979.

TABLE OF CONTENTS

Preface

by Fr. Joseph Towle, S.J.

I believe the most meaningful commendation I could make of Doug's teaching, contained here in the first volume of his Trinity Collection, is that: "It works!" I mean that in no crass sense. He has not sought to provide the reader with some manual for self-improvement, a "how-to" book that guarantees spiritual results if only one follows directions. He knows well how all is grace.

Yet there is so much in the scriptural story of God's free gift to us in Jesus that promises a "power at work in us," a power meant to be displayed not just in words of faith but with the manifestation of the Holy Spirit and appealing signs. I have seen such signs in Doug's ministry, especially with the young — the working of grace. He writes then about that grace "at work," how he has learned of its working and come to expect its working in his own life — and yours.

One of his key understandings is that faith centers on a "living word." It is akin to the Lord Jesus' appealing to John: "Tell John what you have seen and heard: the blind see...to them." John, he knew, would instinctively recognize the prophet's word made flesh in Jesus and in his dungeon womb again make a joyful leap of faith in Him.

For Jesus was indeed the living word making flesh all the depths and beauty of the Hebrew tradition, bringing to a fullness the expectations of the Law and the Prophets. This, Doug writes, to be a living word for this and every age, rendering present in no less striking fashion "a creative energy, a transforming Force, a Spirit that HAS to change the world." Did the Lord not say, "The things that I do, you yourselves shall do — and greater than these shall you do"?

Yet that irresistible Spirit, that very living sharing of union with the Father in Christ and the power inherent in that relationship has been missed — we must confess — by masses of people in the churches. The very "explosive content and core of the Christian Gospel and of Christian faith which it was the intent of Paul, the Saints or the early Church to offer us" has expertly been defused and rendered non-volatile, with tragic consequences for the individual and for the world.

Faith seen and known, in Doug's developing images, as food, living bread and living word does not give such confident assurance of dullness, like a dud in the British War Museum. Doug's own life which he shares with us most openly reveals a faith that is transforming, alive and active. For example, he witnesses to how he was drawn through the very human dialectic of fear, diminishment and failure to know "the healing which is the Father" and to understand the vivid difference between saying the words of faith and living them.

Perhaps there is a special value in the added fact that Doug writes explicitly as a Catholic Christian. There are examples enough in Catholic history to suggest that, as with the Law and the Prophets of Jesus' day, the most living, pulsing traditions can become sedated and trivialized in any given age. And when that happens, what a loss to everyone who considers himself or herself a lover of Jesus. If he writes then — with a certain Pauline urgency — to bear witness to what he has seen and heard of God's power within his own, the Catholic tradition, it should not but help everyone to rejoice: "Does it matter? Grace is everywhere!"

And grace abounds in the fruits of Doug's teaching. Beyond

the sense that his literary effort, as John Calvin might put it, rings with Gospel truth and bears a stamp of personal honesty and humility, the lives of young Catholics he guides grant credibility to his approach to faith. For one who has "seen and heard" the working of grace in the lives of young people Doug works with, the evidence is encouraging— even compelling. The finger of God is here. It is simply not common to observe in teenagers and young adults such felt hunger for God as they have — love of prayer, longing for knowledge, seeking for direction, deep sacramental life, purity of heart, resistance to unexamined peer pressure (John's "overcoming the world"), readiness, transformation, openness to community built on Jesus, simplicity, too, about God and the gifts of the Spirit and — withal — a beautiful deepening of their humanity.

Nothing is the same anymore. God becomes more and more the air they breathe; faith is food. Friendship with the Lord and His mother comes as natural as a high school dance — even moreso. I will always remain touched by the description a fifteen-year old boy gave me of his long bike-rides, spent just talking with Jesus and Mary and crying with joy over the deepening discovery of their love for him, and his for them. He is not an exception among hundreds of "kids," mostly from "public" schools — if that matters — who continue to persevere in their search for God. They witness without fear or affectedness, they struggle to discern what God wants of them, they often enough pay the price for being out of step with the world around them. They love the Eucharist and, I would say, life itself (indeed, perhaps they don't bother making that distinction) — but not in the same way as before.

It is mostly because of them and their love for Doug and what he has helped them discover, that I am confident in recommending this book and those that are to follow.

The Heart Of Christianity —
An Introduction

What on earth is "Faith" all about? A thousand times a year I hear about Catholic people, Christian people, who are of "good Faith." But when I look at their lives, I find myself asking, "Well, what does that statement mean?"

The problem does not stop here. I hear complaints all the time from people who think the Church is no longer "teaching the Faith." When I ask what they mean by "Faith" their answer is unclear. They sound confused, ambiguous, bloated, like me if I were to talk about health food or how to be a "quarterback."

It is somewhat the same with people who justify their non involvement in parish adult education efforts by declaring that they already "know their Faith." When I urge them to tell me of their "Faith," they tell me something that sounds like a Kohlberg Psychology text, only garbled, or like a mixture of popular "wisdom" borrowed from Alan Alda, Archie Bunker, and "The Fonz."

I have often been asked to be part of a "Faith-experience," and yet the experience was not much of anything, never mind "Faith." It was certainly not an experience which would have converted the Roman Empire, or anything like an experience for which the Apostles might have left their home and all that they owned.

In all this I would imply that the problem of what "Faith" is seems to plague even the educators, even the people directing

iv

never seems to go beyond values and principles. It always stays at the level of a moral effort, an effort "... to provide each young person with the opportunity for a life directed by gospel norms," an effort to lead them to "... a personhood formed in the image of Christ..."

Is that all there is to "teaching the Faith"? These words and values expressing "our Faith" are surely not wrong, but they never go quite far enough, or the emphasis never seems to be in the right place. I especially felt that way one time when I was at a first Communion procession. Each child in the procession carried a cross with the American flag stapled right where I would expect the figure of Jesus to be. Perhaps in all of this I'm the one "missing the trick" or I'm the person that needs one more link in my chain to truly understand? Yet, I don't really think so.

And thus I find myself haunted today with the question of what "Christian Faith" is. Sometimes I actually feel like screaming out at some boring "day of recollection" or insipid campus retreat, "Will somebody please tell me what 'Christian Faith' is?" Is it really just a deeper penetration of Ericson or Kohlberg or the Behavioral School? Is it really just "knowing yourself," or knowing you're a good person and worth something because God way "out there somewhere" really loves you? Is Faith only a deeper grasp of "self-actualization" theories or Existentialist philosophy?

And these "Faith-statements" which circulate so freely today, are they telling us all there is to "Faith" when they give us only gospel norms for world peace, the brotherhood of all men, and social justice?

And the "Faith" which sees Jesus only as the American dream, which joins Jesus and the cross to the Red, White and Blue as if they were one and the same — do these American Catholic practices really express all that my Christian Faith is saying?

I don't think so. I do not think there is a "critical bolt" that I am missing. But I do think there is a severe deficiency, even a sharp cleft and division between so much of what I hear and see today, retreats and parish renewal efforts. Catholic school after Catholic school makes public statements about what it is to "communicate the Faith" to our young. They are useful documents to me, and they speak of the beautiful purpose of Catholic Education. However the purpose and what Faith should really mean.

In fact, even for a multitude of Catholic and Christian lives Faith has become drained of life and fullness. It expects little and builds on sand.' It has become cheap "glass" and not a pearl of great price.² It has become something plastic in the true tradition of so many in 20th century America who will cut every corner and compromise high quality to "save a buck" or earn a dollar. It is Faith that has become chemical and synthetic, imitation and substitute, more and more the only choice in our land of famine.³

Christian Faith

Look at what Christian Faith should really mean. It should mean miracles.⁴ It should mean the extraordinary becoming the ordinary every day. It should mean an ancient Word becoming fleshy now and in our own time. It should mean the new dawn of an ancient dream.⁶ It should mean the dream of God walking the streets of our cities in our own day,' of Peter walking on water today before our very eyes.⁸ It should mean people flocking to churches as if they were handing out enormous amounts of money in the middle of the Mass — in fact, for centuries, at the center of the Mass, the Lord has been handing out something worth so much more — so much more than wealth can buy, so much more than man can give.⁹

Faith should mean the sight of poor people rejoicing,¹⁰ the blind receiving their sight, the lame rising up in the embrace of a Power that heals. It should mean a wedding banquet for the poor, the blind, the maimed and the lame." It should mean that we lift our eyes and see a whirling Fire cast down from heaven.¹² It should mean a second flood¹³ unleashed with the force of a tidal wave, consuming the earth with Love.

Christian Faith should mean a "Thanksgiving feast," and a book on Christian Faith should not be anticipated with loathing or reluctance as some arid theological journal, or as a meal of insipid, dried out "left-overs" from days ago. No, that book should mean a "feast"¹⁴ to come, a feast reaching out to a deep hunger in the people of today; a feast too where it will never be a sin to eat more than you should. In fact, it is more strange, but the more you eat the deeper your hunger will grow; the more you drink, the deeper your thirst for a healing spring.¹⁵

And why is all of this true? Because Christian Faith is the Life of Jesus.' Christian Faith is the experience of Jesus living and having His being in God, in a total union of movement with a loving Father.² Faith is the experience of Jesus the Son leaping into the arms of His Father and going wherever the Father would lead.³ Faith is the experience of Jesus knowing' His Father as a real experience, as real as electricity, fire, and the power of Love. Faith is the experience of Jesus knowing His Father *present to Him'* *as* a Love and Power that transformed,⁶ healed, and gave as a gift the courage to be free. Faith is the experience of Jesus knowing as real a Father Who reaches out to us and draws us' to His intimacy and embrace with a Love for us beyond all reason.

Faith is the experience of Jesus striving with all the heart and soul and spirit and strength to know the Father as God,⁸ that is, to know Him as the central goal and critical focus for the effort and striving of each day, each year, as the quest of a lifelong struggle and journey. Faith is the experience of Jesus drawing Life· and strength from God His Father, drawing Life and strength from a Real Presence of Infinite Love for Him. Faith is the heart of Jesus entering into and becoming one with the heart of God, His Father, so much so that in a sense Jesus no longer lives, but only the Father". In the experience of Jesus, the perfection and goal of Christian Faith reveals itself — God becoming flesh" as a fact of Human existence and history.

And the essence of my Christian Faith, the miracle and feast of Christian Faith, is that God draws me into this experience of Jesus." God gives to me the Life and experience of Jesus. As the gift of God, the experience of Christian Faith becomes the experience of Christ's Life and Fire with me and in me." I enter into His Life. His experience becomes my own. I touch the experience of Jesus. In Him, in the Spirit of the Son, I touch the experience of being a child in the arms of a loving Father Whom I know ⸴ as Someone really present to me, as Love and Power that transform" and heal. This experience of Faith is "the feast"⸴ for the blind and lame. It is the embrace of Power that raises the dead to Life." It is the intimate Love that dissipates fear and destroys her chains," the Love that releases joy in the heart of the poor," the Love that gives as a gift a peace no wealth can buy."

This experience is what Christian Faith should really mean. It is the experience of our lives penetrated with the ever-deepening reality of God's Love in the Person of Christ's Spirit.' It is the experience of entering into the radical fact of His Love,² a Love and Spirit longing to be present to us, if we would but open ourselves to receive Him.³

PART I

THE PROBLEM:
To Proclaim Power That
Leads To Faith

Words can release God's power and this power is the foundation of Faith. The experience of Faith cannot live except in the experience of this Power, as the body cannot live apart from the soul and spirit.

"...and my speech and my message were... in demonstration of the Spirit and power that your Faith might rest... in the power of God.."

- 1 Cor. 2:2-5.

Chapter 1

A Basic Idea Of Christian Faith

Christian Faith, as an Experience Seen in its
"Child-Like" Stage or "Starting from Scratch," is
not Essentially Different from the Experience
of Faith One Sees Exemplified in Human Life.

We can see Faith all around us in the simple scenes of human life. I will never forget Bob Richards' real-life story of "Woofer- man,"* the German schoolteacher who threw the javelin over 296 feet in the Munich Olympics. Cheered on by 80,000 countrymen, he beat out his Russian competitor on his third throw by a few centimeters. What proves so amazing though is that before he walked into that stadium crowded with his own people, he had never thrown a javelin over 279 feet.

In a true sense as the event is analyzed it unfolds as a classic example of "love's embrace" calling forth from within, healing, freedom from fear, supreme confidence, and the strength "to dream the impossible dream." The crowd chanting "Wooferman, Wooferman..." really became a sign and reflection of what the Father's Love truly was in the Life of Jesus and what that Love was for all the Christian Saints as well.' The crowd chanting and cheering, charged Wooferman with the experience, or should I say, the "electricity" of Faith. They called his soul to Life, vitality, and power, as truly as the embrace of the Father called Jesus forth to the supreme Love of the Passion.² The crowd's "embrace" moved Wooferman,

---

*I am adapting a true story here which I have heard presented by Bob Richards. The story as presented by him however, served a different purpose and goal.

and drew him to the strength that dissipates fear and destroys her chains.'

Wooferman's first throw was 283 feet. The crowd went wild — he had broken his own record. The crowd stood, clapped, and cheered, and when Wooferman began the next run with javelin poised and ready to fly, the crowd chanted Wooferman's name with accelerating speed as he ran faster and faster. Clearly their support and enthusiasm became for him a call to dreams and vision. In their embrace he could open himself to the miraculous. He could begin to see what he believed of real light just beyond the horizon ready to rise upon his darkness. With each throw his heart moved deeper and deeper into regions that only Faith can experience and to which only Love can lead. Ultimately, the crowd's "embrace" was crucial to his victory.

On Wooferman's third throw, the javelin flew 296 feet and 3 centimeters to win the event and the gold medal. A crowd 80,000 strong — mostly his German country men — were completely overcome with *amazement. They had seen the miraculous; they had seen Faith,* the experience of a man made whole, strong, complete, in a real way perfected and delivered from fear,² in love's embrace.³

Example after example can be seen in human experience of Faith as this sense of life, healing, strength, and freedom born dynamically when we enter love's embrace.⁴ With each witness I become more deeply convinced that we speak of power beyond what we can ask or imagine⁵ when we begin to speak of Christian Faith in the same way. This is really to speak of Christian Faith as the experience of Jesus⁶ — really, as an entering into His experience,' the supreme experience, the unparalleled experience of a Child, a Son, Who was whole and strong and free in the embrace of a Father's Love.⁸

I remember some time ago another example of Faith at the closing of a beautiful weekend event in Christian Community. I choose this particular example because the experience of Faith it captures so effectively was for the girl involved her first experience of Christian Faith as well. The event unfolded when this young girl of about eighteen stood trembling before a group of over a hundred people. She wanted to express her joy and thanksgiving for the love she had shared with us by

2

singing a song — but there was a condition: we would have to sing along during each chorus.

The group as a whole responded and as we sang, there was a sense or discernment clearly communicated to us by her, that she *believed* our love was present and this love was for her; it was embracing her. You might say that the group had truly and authentically become a Mass for her — they had become a sign and source of the Father's Love present for her to experience and know as her own.'

There was also clearly present to us in her what I would call the decisive dimension of Faith — a decision to believe! There was clearly a receptivity and openness to our love reaching out to her. She had clearly chosen to receive and embrace the love extended to her, and actually, how could anyone even speak of Faith as an experience of love's embrace if they will not yield to an embrace or receive it as something to become their own. There is clearly the need for a decisive dimension to Faith, and this dimension of decision and receptivity was vividly present in this young girl so consumed with the embrace of our love.

With each word she sang she seemed to effuse with that love, in a real sense to "...live, and move, and have (her) being..."[3] in union with that love. The girl's face was radiant with joy; her voice, resonant and even angelic in beauty. It was incredible to realize that this was her first solo presentation. And yet she was not alone. I cannot divorce this fullness and vitality, her sense of life, strength, healing and freedom from the embrace of our love.

In fact, you might also say that on this weekend she began to see that her whole life was not a solo presentation. She began to experience Christian Faith, to know the embrace of a deeper Love reaching out to her in and through our love. In fact, it was on this weekend that she began to see what a Son said long before her, "Never am I alone, for always my Father is with me.."[4] On this weekend experience, she began to see that her Life and power and freedom were born only in union with Love, only in the experience of Love's embrace, the embrace of a Father's Love in Christ[3] — the experience that exemplifies Christian Faith. As she sang, Love embraced her in the Person of Christ's Spirit through our community present to her, and her song in this first experience of Christian Faith, whatever song it was or could have been, was really a song of freedom, deliverance, life and joy.

Her decisive freedom also gave anyone present a clear realization that this real Love generated in God and known to Faith was for each of us like food' critical to our strength and wholeness. Perhaps only an example in sharp contrast to this event can portray the critical and foundational nature of this Love. Unfortunately, I have experienced in my own life precisely such a contrast, an occasion where the hostility and true sense of hate present persuaded me to make my remarks brief, to the point, and terminated most expeditiously.

It was an incident in 1971 when I first assumed a role as a Director of Religious Education for a whole Catholic parish. During the first two weeks of catechism classes under my direction, I noted that about three-quarters of my kindergarten teachers, girls in senior high school, were dressing in "mini-skirts" of the shortest length allowed by any and all norms of modesty. Blue-jean commercials were nothing compared to these. I felt that this situation occasioned an announcement addressed to all teachers. I then assembled them after class one Sunday morning and delivered a brief address initiating the immediate implementation of a "dress code" for all teachers.

As I spoke I could sense hostility growing by the moment. I had planned my remarks to be brief — in fact, they were much more brief than I had intended. There were no questions afterwards, and I wanted very much for someone to say something, for a stone-like silence stifled the whole room. I was not free. In fact, I was becoming less free every moment. For awhile I began to wonder if I would ever succeed in this plan, and if so, whether it was to be only at the price of my life. In the end I did get my way and morality was restored at the Sunday school. But after this experience in delivering that address, I can assure you beyond all possibility of doubt that *the embrace of real Love* we receive in Christian Faith gives birth to our healing, strength, and freedom, while its absence can only cripple, destroy, and reduce us to impotence.[2]

Chapter 2

Faith Is Decision

The Decisive Dimension of Faith,
"Do We Choose the Hand of the Father?"

To more deeply grasp what Faith is in all the fullness and richness of its meaning, one has to concentrate on the decisive dimension of Faith. Faith is decision.' I mean by this the fact that people cannot enjoy the experience of Faith unless there is in them a receptivity to the Love that reaches out to them. An authentic experience of Faith builds on a decision to receive divine Love, to receive the Father's Spirit Who calls us to union with God. This receptivity is the crucial essence of believing. People can never come to a mature experience of Faith as an entering into the Life of Jesus without this decisive receptivity.

Even when we look at the experience of God present to the early Church in the power of Christ's Spirit, what essentially are the charismata of which the Scripture so clearly speaks?[2] What are these powerful gifts of the Spirit, through which Jesus Risen made His Presence so alive and so deeply experienced to them who first *believed Him,* to them who first *received* the Spirit of His Love?[3] These gifts seen in their essential reality are forms of loving activity,[4] supernatural forms of loving service poured out upon men and women who had entered into divine Love,[5] and who in this Love had dedicated themselves to building up and caring for the Body of Christ on earth, the Church."

But to be as clear and plain as possible, perhaps even crude, why would we need a bat, a glove, and a ball, if we were not at all interested in baseball? Why would we need the charismata, or why would we experience God present in power in the gifts of His Love, the gifts of His Spirit, if our hearts were cold or closed to Love? An unloving people has no need of the charismata, and such a people does not experience God' present in power as the transforming Love that is His Spirit.² But were that people to enter Love, to receive Love, to open their hearts to Love, to decide for Life in Christ, to believe,' then God in the power of His gifts and in the Person of His Love can once again come to earth in the rush of a mighty Wind and unquenchable Fire.⁴

There is a need then to attach critical importance to this fact — that for the experience of Faith in all of its fullness we have to decisively embrace Love. Having the experience of Christ that is real Faith, the Life of Jesus that is Christian Faith,' builds on a decision to embrace Love. This decisive dimension of Faith is an essential imperative. This decision to embrace Love has to be inherently included in the experience of Faith or necessarily at the heart of the experience, or Faith cannot be real. It can only be a delusion or a lie.

How is real Faith possible otherwise without this element of decision? How can we speak of real Faith without this deliberate movement on our part toward embrace and union with a God Who is a Father's Love(' reaching out to us and calling us in Christ to enter into Him?' When we speak of Christian Faith in its essential character as the experience of Jesus, as really an entering into the experience of this Man whose Life is the embrace of a Father's Love, then we have to speak of Faith as having a decisive dimensnion — that is, as an experience man cannot have but for the decision to embrace a Father's Love *with Jesus and in Jesus.* The experience of Faith as entering into Christ's Life and touching His experience can only occur if we allow ourselves to "leap" with Him into the Father's arms, only if we receive with Him the embrace of His Father's Love, only if we decide to live and have our being with Jesus in a total union of movement with His Father's Love'

Perhaps I could enhance or magnify this decisive quality so intrinsic to the real experience of Faith through an example that is

6

repeated again and again in my experience with my own children. It is the kind of experience that most often happens at amusement parks at a ride like the Alpine Chair Lift, or even more so when they catch a first glimpse of an ominous ride such as the Witch's Castle (a fun house at a neighboring beach here). There's usually a dragon or a moving witch somewhere above the entrance, and it becomes my job (the Father) to lead my children on through the entrance, in faith they will be safe *despite what they see.'* I extend my hands to them and speak to them. My words and my outstretched arms invite them to embrace me, and in my embrace I hope to encourage and assure them, to fortify them *and allay their fear.* It then becomes their task *to choose.* They can take hold of my hands and enter into my embrace; they can believe my word and move to find shelter in my presence, or they can embrace the fear.

There is also a parallel to this experience in the gospels where the Lord invites Peter to walk upon the water.' Does Peter choose the strength of Christ's outstretched arm and the power of His words and Presence? Really, does he choose to embrace the Lord and be one with Him in that moment, or does he embrace the turbulence, the storm, the darkness? Does he choose to embrace the Lord revealing a Father's Love, or embrace the fear excited by formidable winds, waves, and clouds?

I also see the same parallel in the Christian life, for what is the event unfolding to our experience every day in the Eucharist if not the Father's outstretched arm in Christ rendered present in the Mass?' The dragon, the witch, and fear in all its forms — they burden, oppress, and raise their ugly heads relentlessly and tirelessly in the storms and struggles of our daily life. But the Father's hand in the Eucharistic Christ reaches out to embrace us with encouragement and assurance; the Father in Christ joins us to Himself to fortify us and to allay our fear.

Still I must choose; Peter must choose; my children must choose. All of us — my children, Peter, myself — all of us, each of us, cannot escape decision and choice. Decision is there and has to be there at the heart of any real experience of Faith, any authentic experience of love's embrace.

Signs of Unbelief in the Christianity of Our Time

Yet questions are very much alive in my mind as I consider the Christianity of our own day: *Do we choose the hand of the Father?'* Do we enter into His embrace? Do we take hold of His outstretched arm, and find shelter in the power of His Presence and His Word to us: "Take Heart, it is I; have no fear"? Or do we embrace the turbulence, the storm, the darkness, and even become the possession of fear itself?

What an art film we could make out of the questions in this one paragraph. They *are a* profound challenge to both the American Church and "Christian American Society" as well. Are we in fact prodigal sons refusing to go where the Father will lead? For me that would certainly seem to be the only conclusion possible if my examples truly depict what is essential to authentic Faith, what it is to decisively embrace Love and surrender to this Power.

In my examples I am seeing an authentic experience of Faith being achieved and realized in the experience of St. Peter on the water, or even in the moment I describe with my own children. It is these moments that describe the genuine experience of Faith, and I would not want to dismiss them lightly as unworthy barometers or faulty gauges unfit to evaluate the real presence of Faith today in our churches or secular world. On the contrary, I think these moments provide an excellent barometer. I think they represent a rich and full expression of what Faith is in its essential substance and core, and I simply love the Faith that these moments describe. Why settle for less than this? Why `!settle for beans" or a cheese sandwich when these moments give us a description of Faith as magnificent as a steak banquet?*

Look once again at these moments. Is it no wonder that I love them and the Faith they describe — especially the moment I remember so well with my children? I loved going through that experience with them. I feel that I shared in that experience something of the delight and excitment of God the Father as men believe — and when precisely did I feel this way? When my children believed, in that powerful moment when my children embraced me, when they took hold of me with a firm grip and then fixed their eyes squarely and sternly on the moving witch and the

---

*This is an analogy drawn from the *Antioch Weekend,* where I heard it used by Patti Gallagher Mansfield. Her own witness to Life in the Spirit has been recorded in a book entitled *Cathlolic Pentecostals.*

snarling dragon. This is the moment when Faith emerged for them as a real experience. This moment is the moment when Peter was rising up in the sea and squarely facing the challenge of the storm through the power of union with Jesus' Presence. This moment is the moment I leave the altar of God having embraced the Body and Blood of Christ, and now filled with fire, zeal, and enthusiasm, I challenge the anxieties, the burdens, and the struggles of my day. At Mass, I choose to become the Bride of Fire, the Spouse empowered in the embrace of God's Spirit.' I choose to become like the Son secure in the embrace of a Father's love. I choose the experience of Faith.

Now evaluate with me the real presence of this Faith today in our Churches and secular society. Where in our Churches and secular world, where in our "Christian culture" is this decisive moment of Faith that the children of God can achieve and realize, and which their God delights to see? Where is the power of that moment in our world today when men embrace the Father, when they take hold of the Father's hand with a firm grip and then fix their eyes squarely and sternly on the moving witch and the snarling dragon? Please be candid and tell me if our American Church and indeed our "Christian American Society" is going freely and without fear where the hand of the Father will lead. It would be difficult for me to believe that we are — that very many among us are in fact going His way at all in any significant degree.

On the contrary, rather too glaring for my eyes to ignore is the sight of malaise and disease — unbelief — infecting our Church and our culture. Rather than any decision to go where the hand of the Father will lead, our Church is "floating downstream" with a dehumanizing society and even attempting to take Christ along. We extend our hands to Him and invite Him to partake of our bondage, but He does not come. Am I overbearing, harsh, exaggerating, too enamored with the histrionic and hyperbole? If we are taking the hand of the Father to the Bold Love He offers, why is the Love of a Mother Teresa such an anomaly in our world?

Why too is there a virtual absence of risk infecting our Church and our "Christian" society? Why the virtual absence of adventure and courage? So many will often ask me what adventure and bold challenge have to do with "being a Catholic" or "being a man of Christian Faith." Yet the *Acts of the Apostles' is* a very clear

9

and compelling witness to the adventure and daring of primitive Christianity, to what happens when a people becomes animated with the zeal of God's Spirit. They are driven irresistibly' to proclaim Christ, to render His Love present in the world with their lives. No risk is too great for them, and nothing can separate them from Christ's Love — "no tribulation, distress, persecution, famine...peril, nakedness, or sword...In all these things they are more than conquerors through Him Who loves us..."[2] The Scripture then is all too clear, in fact, even void in ambiguity concerning the difference before and after Pentecost, the difference in the lives of a people who have known the outpouring of God's Love and Presence upon them.[3]

Yet I wonder seriously if what I see today in our culture and even our Churches more truly represents the experience before the Pentecost event. For where today is the zeal of the Acts, or the lives of Paul and the Saints, the enthusiasm of the early Church that seized Christians, empowering them to face the challenges of Love and the adversity of Life? Instead, why today the escape, the boredom, the depression, the emptiness, "the loveless toil we fill our days with"?* Why the mass proliferation of escape mechanisms — sexual perversion, drug addiction, alcoholism, orgiastic dance — even among the supposedly baptized?

If we are rising to Bold Love, why then in the light of years and years of experience with people in parish work do I experience what should never be experienced in the lives of Christian people supposedly brought up in the intimacy and embrace of God's profound Love? What I experience even among them is an obsession of social dimensions, a contemporary obsession with working, doing, performing toward the achievement of some sense of worth and importance — even at the expense of prayer, peace of mind, mental balance, intimacy with spouse, children, and friends. I do believe it is precisely because even among supposed believers there is unbelief, the absence or perhaps the rejection of the Father's embrace, really, of Love's embrace.[4] It is exactly because underlying all of our anxious toil we find

*This is a line spoken by Francis of Assisi in the film, "Brother Sun, Sister Moon."

10

present, even among Christians, the universal experience that characterizes man steeped in unbelief and distant from Love. This experience all- pervasive among men without Faith is the experience that no man can stand or long endure — it is the feeling that we are unloved, worthless to anyone or everyone. And today even among countless Christians, there is deeply present this feeling that we are in fact unloved.

In the pain of that experience, men, even Christians, desperately search for a substitute "Bread". They settle for a surrogate, for the anxiety-ridden behavior of the 20th century. They settle for doing, relentlessly working, performing, achieving — all toward some sense of worth which they do not feel in their distance from the experience of true prayer which is *the experience of Faith — the experience of openness, surrender, and receptivity to the outstretched hands of a Loving Father.* It is the sense of worth impossible to achieve in separation from the Love Who is God alone' and the Love of His people imbued through Faith with His transforming Spirit.[2] It is the sense of worth, value, and fulfillment that only a Father's Love can give.[3] A John Paul, a Mother Teresa, all the Saints, every "child" in the arms of the loving Father knows the sense of worth and importance of which I speak. They know their dignity and importance beyond what wealth can measure or what a dictionary can define.[4] It is the sense of value born only in the embrace of a loving Father Whom they know as real[5] to their experience, only in the embrace of a Father truly present to them in power[o] as a Love beyond all reason, beyond all they can ask or imagine.'

11

Chapter 3

The Experience of God's Love Is Real

Modern man is truly craving for this sense of meaning, worth, and fulfillment known only to the man of Faith. It is a sense of fulfillment, wholeness, and completion known only to this man who chooses to enter the experience of Faith.' It is a fulfillment known only to this man who in a real way becomes "child", like a "Child" or a Son long ago. For this man only, a sense of wholeness and fulfillment, a sense of completion, healing and freedom emerge dynamically precisely because he enters into the experience of Jesus. It is the experience of this "Child" or Son long ago, the experience of the only Son Who believed, the Son Who was open and receptive totally to the Love of a Father longing to be present to all men with infinite Love.

Now there is something further here to underscore that is of critical importance to understand the experience of Christian Faith in all the fullness of its meaning. All along here I presume the fact and reality of this divine Love that reaches out to men. I presume there is this Love ready and longing to intervene decisively in our lives for the price of our openness and receptivity. Yet for the price of our decision to receive it and embrace it, for the price of our openness, it is precisely crucial at this point to emphasize and underscore that this Love is a fact — it is there' and wants to intervene in our lives for the price of Faith.

And I cannot begin to say how crucial it is that we underscore this fact of a Father's Love as a real experience for the man who believes, for this man who opens to receive an infinite Love that

12

truly reaches out to him.' I would really want to stress as explicity as possible that this is an extremely important fact with extraordinary ramifications. We are dealing with a fact nothing less than critical to the heart and essence of Christian Faith when we speak of Faith as a *real experience* of God's Love, as an encounter with a living Father *Who authentically becomes present to me* in Faith, as an encounter with Someone Who longs to reveal His Love for me so that my heart can see His Love and knows the Love that is His Spirit as *present and real to my experience.*

To object to this fact of a Father's Love as a real experience for the man of Faith is to undermine the essential significance of God becoming man.ᴴ It even further undermines the essential significance of the Father in Christ sending forth His Spirit upon men toward the creation of Church, the creation of Church as the Body of Jesus continuing to be alive and present upon the earth.'

But all of these considerations lead me away from my fin- mediate objective — only to establish the fact of a Father's Love as a real experience for the man of Faith. And I want to underscore this fact particularly in the light of objections that are raised especially as I use the examples of Faith that have been employed thus far (e.g., my children at the amusement park, Peter walking on the water). I would see these examples as experience which exemplify what Christian Faith truly is in its substance and foundation. Yet some will say in the light of them that it is fine to talk about St. Peter receiving the outstretched arm of Christ,' or about my children taking hold of my hand, or about a young girl being embraced by a community's love for her — in all these instances there is something real you can bite into, something you can receive, open yourself to, something you can believe in. But God's Love? What on earth or beyond the earth are you talking about?

Yet I would contend most strongly that this Love is a fact, a fact ready and longing to intervene decisively in our lives. If only we receive, open ourselves to embrace this Love reaching out to us, if only we believe, we shall in fact behold the power of God,' the Spirit that is His Love.

With the clear acceptance of this fact, we begin to let "Faith" come of age or begin to see Christian Faith in a full and comprehensive way. This is to speak of it as the experience of Jesus,

13

really as an entering into the experience of the Son Who knew wholeness, perfection, and freedom in the embrace of the Father's Love. The experience of Christian Faith has really nowhere else to go! — no other point really to strive for, no other point really as its summit and perfection — either I can or can't talk about the fact of a Father's Love as real to my experience, as my real experience of Faith. And if I can then I need irresistibly to proclaim what I have seen and heard, the real experience of Faith seen and known as the Life of Christ in me, and as my real encounter and union with the Father's Love in that Life.

As a paradigm and model of what Faith is, seen in this way, I would share one last example from my own childhood. It is an incident to which I always come back to express and capture for myself the essence of what Christian Faith is as my real experience of the Father's Love in Christ.

It is an incident of my early youth which I remember vividly and which even now can move me to the point of tears, but tears truly born of joy. My father and I had a race. He challenged me — if I thought I could run so fast, why shouldn't I try to beat him? We ran around our block. We ran down Spruce Street, and turned left on Park Street, and then began our return down Well Street. I would look at my Dad every so often an especially toward the end of the race. There was sheer delight in his face. He beamed with pride over his son. He was letting me win, *but knowing and seeing so clearly his love for me* I cannot begin to tell you the joy welling up within my heart. I was loved by my father. I was the delight of my father. When I had won the race he picked me up and embraced me. And my joy in that moment could have conquered all struggle, adversity, trial, and suffering.'

Simply put, this singular moment has become a graphic description, in metaphor if you will, of the experience of Christian Faith, of what it is to live each day of my life in the arms of God. *I* am a *child in the arms of my Loving Father.* The secret to all joy and bliss during and beyond the course of our fragile earthly existence is to be nothing more or less than this — a child in the loving embrace of God, *to apprehend* through prayer and Eucharist the outstretched arms of a Loving Father reaching down to me in Jesus lest I sink in a sea of storms. It is worth any price I can pay for that joyous moment of my Father's embrace to be my

14

constant experience. My whole life has in fact become a struggle and challenge to come to that experience of Faith, to that experience of the Father's Love as to the God of my Life.' This means that I move toward the experience of His Love as toward the goal for the effort and striving of each day, each month, each year. The Spirit of His Love becomes the focus and term even of my life-long journey.' He becomes my Heart,' the Feast at the heart of each day, the Bread of my life' and my Living Water' in a land of famine; my Home,' Healing,' and Freedom,' the Pearl given freely yet worth more than any price I have ever paid. And yet why weigh the,price for the Life I could never earn, for the Life that is God Himself?"

Chapter 4

The Experience Of Christian Faith
A Son In The Arms Of A Loving Father

When you begin to see the experience of Faith in all the fullness and richness of its meaning, a sense and vision of force and power is inescapable.' It is like thinking that a cheese sandwich* was all there was and then finding out a steak dinner was the real fare. It is like thinking that a kiss was the summit moment, but then finding out that there is intercourse as well.

In attesting to the truth of all this, I can only bear witness to what I have seen and heard of God's Love penetrating to the very depths of my life. What follows now is nothing more or less than this — the experience of Faith as I have known it; the Presence of God "breathing," reaching deeply into my life, and providing an authentic experience of being the Son secure and protected and strong in the powerful embrace of God.

Financial Massacre

In my recent experience, a significant moment that I would share is a moment that came a few years ago in the face of an overwhelming onslaught of depression stemming from the loss of all my savings in a security venture.

It is not to the point to discuss the circumstances precipitating such a loss. They were freakish and arbitrary, and the loss itself was devasting. It is more to the point here to note that over half

---

*This is a second reference to an analogy drawn from the *Antioch Weekend* mentioned already on P.8

16

the loss occurred in a matter of hours on a Friday afternoon while I was in preparation for a retreat. *I was to lead* the retreat geared to high school and college youth, and furthermore I went into the retreat fully cognizant of losses I would have to sustain. I can only think of a tidal wave threatening to crush mel when I ponder the fear, insecurity, and darkness that engulfed me in that hour. Shackles threatened to bind me in that moment, and weakness plagued me through the whole first night of my retreat until the hours just before the dawn. Many perhaps have experienced a similar assault, and perhaps the loss — being that of a wife, a son, a daughter, a home, a country, a friend — is of a nature that dwarfs mine by comparison.

But all I need to say here is that my trembling was real, my fear real, my chains very real. How I prayed that night for focus, for concentration on the Person of Jesus Who alone is Life and Joy, and not on money. How I prayed for deliverance, redemption, for a Spirit that could be joyous and free in God and indifferent to money. My prayer was deep; I used the Jesus prayer, for me a constant crying out with the names of Jesus and Mary. I experienced in myself the deceit, the sham, the ludicrous masquerade of claiming indifference to money while my heart could only rest securely while amassing wealth and "building bigger barns." Strip it away and where was my joy in God? Where was my freedom and happiness because I am a child in the arms of God my Loving Father? Yet I knew there was a gift of freedom and wisdom being given to me through this trial...

I tossed and turned, tired and sleepless until around four thirty a.m., repeating always the names of Jesus and Mary. I prayed with all my heart for the coming of the Power Who alone could release me from the chains threatening to bind me. I prayed for the coming of the Spirit Who alone could withstand the force of a tidal wave larger than my weak flesh could resist. And then for the price of my ceaseless prayer, the Power of the Spirit overshadowed me." The Father embraced me. My prayer had prepared me for a deep experience of Faith. It was the prayer of a child believing that the Father alone was the source of his joy and Life. It was the prayer of the Son crying out to *Him* alone, the Son turning the focus of his heart from the darkness and its snares, and guarding it for the

17

possession and embrace of God alone." It was the prayer of the child believing as he cries, that the Father longs to come to him in his nightmare, that the Father longs to embrace him, comfort him, and restore him to peace.'

This is precisely what happened to me in my living nightmare, even as the darkness gave way to the dawn during the first night of my retreat. What did I experience? There was a sense of euphoria, exaltation. There was an excessive, overwhelming feeling of comfort and well-being that had absolutely no grounds for its existence. But more than this, there was as well the consolation of joy that consumed me. There was a sense of what I experienced that day running with my father. I was free in the overwhelming experience that God loved me. His Love embracing me absorbed the whole of my attention, and in the joy of such piercing Light, my heart became blind to all other care. There was a sense of being embraced by an all-powerful Love rendering me secure and at peace when there was no reason for peace. There was a sense of being caught up and rapt in God — a sense of being apprehended by my Father. He was reaching out to His child ensnared and consumed by a nightmarish vision. Divine, transcendant Power surged into its earthen vessel. Though afflicted in every way, I could not be crushed *in Him;* struck down I could not be destroyed *in Him.'* Despair could have no power over me.

When I jogged a little while later in the early morning sun, I was running around my block again as a boy with my Father. His Love embracing me was everything. I had nothing, but possessed everything. I was filled with a longing to give this Love and be this Love for others, to be His healing Love for a world so desperately in need of it. I began to dream of a Catholic and Christian Church which would be in each of its members a source of this Father's healing Love for a sick world drowning in its own pride and folly.

PART II

For all who believe,
the power at the heart
of Christianity

The Ann Arbor Experience
*"Jesus said to her, 'Did I not tell you that
if you would believe you would see the power of God...'"*

- Jn. 11:40

Chapter 1

A Journey Into The Night

*The Pivotal Experience of Christian Faith,
of What It Is to Enter the Life of Jesus and to
Become in Him the Son Knowing the Father's Love.'*

My experience in Ann Arbor happened long ago just after graduating from four great years at Holy Cross College. The experience began in such a way that seemed too good to be true — and it was. The way I saw it in my own fantasy, I was still extremely young and yet I had already achieved a spectacular rise to an acknowledged and authorized leadership position in a very important community, a community which even at that time was commanding national attention. With only a B.A. in Theology- Philosophy, armed with the Spirit of God, and working closely with brothers committed to me in love, it seemed like the renewal of the Church in Christ and the conquest of America through His power was a matter of destiny.

It was a dream that would unfold for us and for me, given that I could wait a couple of years. There was a real sense of being carried along by the crest of a wave which knew only "success," but really a false "success" that could only mean the triumph of good and grace as precluding the experience of trial, hardship, desolation, and defeat.' But the crest of a wave does not last forever, and a time was coming when I would learn that my baptism was not the price of an easy life, but the gift of power to face challenge and adversity, the gift to stay afloat in a storm at sea.'

The time came too soon, and it came as the flowering of my own mistakes and foolishness. It was the product of poor decisions and perhaps some measure of presumption. In the course of one year's time I had "progressed" to the point where the anxiety and the nervous tension in my life were unbearable. I had not foreseen the stress of responsibility and the pressure of an endless schedule larger than any I had ever been accustomed to and greater than any I should ever have assumed. God had called me to peace. I had craftily plotted the safest road to nervous exhaustion.

It is not difficult to describe how it came about. As I have already said, it was a "flowering" of seeds that had been planted all along the way. These were the seeds of my ultimate defeat, seeds growing into the failure of my quest to become a "more than human" apostle. The crux of the problem was that the quest was my ambition, but not God's gift.' I had decided for the quest, but not God. It would be like deciding to perform miracles or deciding to do a Katherine Kuhlman healing service yet without the anointing of the Spirit.* And irrespective of this, there was a sense of "proceeding boldly" at that.

These reflections incisively describe an overview of my experience. I had decided to become Christ's Love for a large number of people who freely and trustingly entered into my care. It was only a short time before I began to discover that becoming Christ's Love, *period,* might mean a much larger investment in foundations for growth' in the Spirit of God than I had ever imagined.

I can see now *the humor* of the Father through all of this period, although it was hard for me to see it then. Even now as a father myself, I often let my children learn one of the most effective ways that they can — by experiencing their own mistakes. So it was during this period of my life. My Father looked on from a distance as I tried to build the dam only after I could see the flood coming. Or perhaps in a more appropriate image, He watched from afar as I searched for roots to Life and Strength in Him,' but only after I had many limbs and branches in the form of many spiritual children — all of them looking to me as a source of water, bread, and nourishment.'

The most chaotic dimension or aspect to my strategy at this

*Concerning the work of Katherine Kuhlman one could refer to the biography of her life by Jamie Buckingham.

time was that *I looked to God in fact as only a means* to something else, and that "something else" was really the focus of my heart and spirit. What was that "something else"? I needed strength. I wanted "spiritual power." My whole quest and dream were in jeopardy, the quest for charism and dynamism in a spectacular ministry responding to the spiritual hunger of a huge number of people. I was becoming tired, emotionally drained, intellectually stagnant, spiritually depressed and deflated. My experience was the weight of a large building on a fragile foundation of a newborn prayer life and an unripened devotion to Eucharist, scripture, and the discipline of fasting and penance.

In a sense, as I reminisce over this situation, what I view is my delinquent, anxious, and belated efforts to become water and roots for a fully-grown tree. In a sense, I began to build a strong foundation under the oppressive weight of a building which already stood. There is an element of humor in all this that looking back now I find difficult to conceal, but at the time there was only the desperation of a man caught in a web and not knowing what to do, or how and where to go.

In this confusion of desperation, I added to my problem. To the weight of unbearable responsibility and a measure of personal contact already proving to sap my strength beyond a doubt, I now combined a zealous effort to enter into penance and prayer, perhaps hoping to become another Cure' of Ars* before the building collapsed. I have no doubt now about the debilitating effect upon my health during this period of poor eating habits and irregular sleep. The Cure' of Ars had lived on the Eucharist, on the strength of the Spirit he embraced in prayer; I would do the same, but with that one little difference I spoke of earlier. I had no clear mandate or sign from God that this was His disposition and pleasure for me, at least not at this point in my life.

In fact, every sign indicated exactly the opposite. The anxiety increased. The tension increased. The stress assumed the form and dimensions of a tidal wave larger than myself, larger than anything I could withstand unaided by grace. But there was still denial of reality and denial of my weakness. "The straw breaking' the camel's back" was yet to come. I needed but one more sign to

*Concerning the person and work of the Cure' of Ars, John Vianney, one could refer to the excellent biography of his life by Francis Trochu.

show me that I was man, not God, to precipitate in my heart a movement of true humility. I needed but one more sign to precipitate in my heart the child's deep awareness of his need for the Love, strength, and protection of his divine Father.'

The sign I needed "ripened" and came to fruition in my "living situation" at the time. I do not say "home" because that is precisely what it was not and precisely why it became that source of stress moving me to the point where afflicted I was crushed, and struck down I was destroyed.² Without realizing it or consciously planning it, I had placed myself on a daily basis in an extremely high stress situation, namely living in a leadership household of the Ann Arbor community.

Basically what that meant for me was a daily drain of adrenal energy. The experience of being in that "home" was for me like the experience of being "on stage" all the days of my life. I could seldom find privacy or the freedom to be be myself. Nor could I find the freedom to rest due to a constant influx of visitors from throughout the nation. They came to live with us, and while doing so proceeded to examine meticulously our living habits, our spiritual life, and any and all "evidence of holiness."

I can't blame these people at all for doing what they did. They were people well-intentioned, excited, and filled with zeal, and the Ann Arbor community* even from its earliest days inspired within them, as well as so many others throughout the country, an awe, a wonder and hope. There was an intense fascination about it as there should have been, and as there should be even to this day. For it was and still is now a prayerful effort to recapture and return to our Christian roots, the dynamism of the early Christian communities of Acts, Corinthians, and all the letters of Paul.³ Irrespective of their good reasons though, I did not have at the time the wisdom of God my Father to handle the deluge of scrutiny and examination to which I was subjected by all these visitors, the "on-stage" feeling of being appraised and evaluated as I sat at a table or "rested" in my living room, or as I dared to sleep a half hour longer.

*For more information on this community, and the exemplary effort at renewal which it represents, I would recommend the book *Building Christian Community* by Steven Clark.

At the Height of Trial

And so the moment came in November of 1969, when I began to experience alarm reactions just at the thought of going home to dinner. There were heart palpitations and a tremor reaction in my hands unlike anything I had ever known. Sometimes at dinner or just in my "home," I would experience a shortness of wind in my lungs like I would before a major talk to a large audience. However, now I was experiencing these things on a regular basis and just as a response to ordinary, harmless stimuli — dinner, conversation, a phone call... My day more than ever demanded strength and endurance beyond what I could summon at will. My whole life-situation was clearly more than I could bear.

As a boy, I had had at times a tremor reaction or a heart palpitation, perhaps &ring a big moment in a baseball game, or whenever I had to speak in public. But now my whole life was "one big moment". The anxiety was all-pervasive and I was truly alarmed. Stress permeated my existence. There was the sense of being constantly inundated — talks to write and more people to see, more than I could ever possibly respond to with proper care and emotion; the demands of leadership responsibility; the constant feeling of being scrutinized in my own "home situation," and even interrogated and angrily challenged by guests if they were antagonized by their Ann Arbor experience. There was the lack of "home" as the home of my youth was home, the lack of sufficient sleep, the lack of a balanced diet, and the lack of friendship as well. I had in fact no time for the loving contemplation of my brothers and sisters. There was for me a sense of constantly "building" the kingdom of God on earth. I felt overwhelmed by a tidal wave larger than any man could withstand unaided by God's power, and the storm which engulfed me in that moment swept easily into the hands of anxious fear.'

Chapter 2

A Light Just Beyond The Horizon

I had begun to seriously attempt fasting, penance, and prayer, and *it was now in prayer that I began to experience a movement toward deliverance.* As part of my effort, I had started to kneel for long periods in prayer late each evening, in the hope that God would heal me and deliver me of my plight. I want to emphasize though that there was a sense here in which God was only a means. There was a sense in which my prayer was not a zealous effort to enter more deeply into God, but a desperate effort to seek the healing of anxiety, God's Light penetrating my confusion, the peace of God overcoming the turbulence of my soul. There was still a sense in which the "cart was before the horse." There was still a sense in which I needed God *in order* to reach my dreams and ambitions. But the whole reality of God as an end in Himself,' as "the pearl of great price,"₂ as "the one thing needful'" was not yet at the heart of my life's work and striving. However, if we enter prayer through the "door" of our own human desire, it is not long before we leave prayer through God's "door," the "door" through which He leads.*

I would now enter prayer anxiously, in darkness, in turbulence, knowing not where else I might go for Life and healing. And gradually as the evenings passed, the Father came to me — He came to His son in his nightmare. It was plain to me that a Presence was there as if surrounding me. There was a sense of Presence leading me to experience consolation, peace, joy moving

*This analogy is borrowed from the thought of St. Ignatius of Loyola.

25

me to tears despite all natural reason for it.[1]

Without my realizing it, the Lord led me out of my evening prayer little by little through His "door," a door unveiling a vision to me that His Presence was everything for *me.'* *He wanted to be the End of my prayer;* the End of my prayer was not to be my dream for healing. *He was my Healing.* He was my Dream, my Ambition, my Quest, the Goal for which I was working, counseling, writing talks, leading retreats. What in fact was also the Dream, the Vision, and the Quest of Francis, John Vianney, all the Saints? For what did they tirelessly work and ceaselessly strive for, if not the Dream of God Himself coming to earth,[3] the Word becoming flesh[4] now, in this time, in this place?

I had not yet realized this dream, but I did begin to leave my evening periods of prayer feeling embraced, loved, and more than this, even *in love.* Without realizing it, I was beginning to change the focus of my life and heart. A Light was dawning and I was in fact being drawn to look and notice, but my change of focus was slight and still beyond my deep awareness.

Perhaps I can best express my whole feeling at this time by comparison to the simple experience of two people falling in love. With myself I can remember distinctly a point in my awareness where I could see only that I was taking notice of a girl, but I would be hard-pressed to believe that my life was indeed changing focus, or that I was "changing" in any way at all. The power of "love" still eluded me, especially the fact that it was taking hold of me or that I was somehow caught in its power. Yet this was only at the beginning of the experience, and so also with the experience of God.

With the coming of change, transformation and repentance, I would clearly become aware. However, for change and repentance that I could see, something more of His Love was needed, but yet to come — the experience of God's Love present to me[3] with power, power undeniable and real, the power of His Love transforming' my Life. You might say that as yet the dawn had not really happened. I was at the point of a kiss, but the experience of transforming union had yet to occur. There was something of Love present, but only the seed of what was to come.

Sufficient to say for now, is that I did experience something of God's Love touching me in prayer, and what I did experience was in reality a vital contact with what I would call the true and authentic experience of Faith, that is, Faith seen as the experience of Jesus, really an entering into His Life.' In my prayer I was coming to His vision and experience of the Father's Love[2] which is the height and essence of authentic Faith. Had it not been for this real sense of intimacy with Jesus truly present in prayer, I would have only seen an assault of evil and the triumph of darkness in November of '69. The fruit of all my labor, onerous and endless, would have been profound trial and defeat. It would have been wounds, hurt, ridicule, and crucifixion. But this was not the case. My commitment to prayer and especially to Eucharist,[3] irrespective of the reasons for which I first made them, proved at this time to be the decisive factor truly thwarting triumph of darkness and failure that I so immensely feared. Up to this point, it was beyond my wildest dreams and not even within my conscious awareness that these simple commitments were feeding me with healing Food;[4] that they were putting me into a real experienced contact with Power that could raise from the dead,' contact with Power that could restore me to health and wholeness, contact with Power that could create something from nothing.°

A deep awareness of all this was yet to come. There was still only a growing vision and a "dawning" experience of the Father's tender Love for me. And *this experience of being loved* is what did begin to grow more and more within my consciousness with each passing day. Despite the darkness engulfing me I became more and more aware of the fact that the Father loved me, and because of a zealous entering into deeper prayer, my heart was growing in strength to *not believe the darkness I could see,* but to deeply see what I had always believed — that God is Love for me.[7]

At this point in my growth, then, because there was strength present to hold fast and sustain this clear vision, this vital experience of a Love for me which the world cannot see,[8] I would have to observe that I was already beginning to touch the true experience of Faith. I was beginning to touch the real experience of Christian Faith, the transforming experience of Jesus in union with Love. Already I was touching His strength; already I was really entering His victory that overcomes the world;[9] already, though without any real deep awareness, I was entering into the strength of the *Son* knowing intimately and totally the embrace

A Light Just Beyond The Horizon

of the Father's Love.'

Chapter 3

The Experience Of Faith
The Vision of His Divine Love

Once in my own present role as father, I was awakened one night by my little girl Claire who was in the middle of a nightmare. It would be good to tell what happened that night to Claire in order to enhance some grasp of my own experience to this point in my story, for I really don't see my own experience as significantly all that different from hers.

She was only two years old at the time, and I remember her clearly crying out, "Daddy!, Daddy!" And what I remember seeing in myself as I rushed to her room practically still in my sleep (I can still feel my foot smashing into an iron bedpost) really captures for me what I began to sense of God's Love in Ann Arbor. Now I know the image is only analogous, but as real as my intense Love was to Clair, so real to mel was the Love in the experience of God my Father, an intense Love touching me with the prayer of each evening. Even as I know that Clair could feel my intense Love, so I know that I could feel this intense Love of the Father for me.

What was it like? It was very much like what I was feeling for Claire. Even as I rushed to Claire's room I could not bear the thought of her pain and torment, small as it might be, and the force of Love surging within me would have paid any price to end her pain.

It was this kind of Love I could sense in prayer, and yet at the same time it was so much more than this Love. It was a kind of

Love I see for me in Jesus on the cross,' or in Mary my mother as she holds her Son in the Pieta. It was the kind of Love that surpasses what natural men can feel or give;' it rises above their Love even as the heavens rise above the earth.' "...For if you, evil as you are, know how to give good gifts to your children, how much more will your heavenly Father..."' It was a Love transcending anything I could be or feel.

Nevertheless, this Love in God for me was real — I was knowing it in the prayer of each night and I was being embraced by it. I was knowing the Love of my Father lifting me up, beaming with joy as He holds me and calls me His own.' I would leave my evening prayer with a sense of really being embraced by God and with a vision of His Love that was truly overwhelming.

There is one further example of what this Love was like and the image is so vivid and forceful that I should share it. I would be remiss to ignore or discard it, for it captures too perfectly the experience of this Presence. It is an image that I have drawn from the film "Ben Hur." I can clearly remember the film, and I can remember Ben Hur's relentless search' for his mother and sister. He finally found them rotting in some hellhole dungeon, reduced to lepers who were denied light, fresh air, food, and any experience of human tenderness and warmth for more than five years. In my evening prayer I would often feel like the mother and sister of Ben Hur — struck down, defeated, imprisoned, afflicted in every way, and engulfed by darkness. But it was as if I grew to know in these deep moments of prayerful embrace with God that *I was in His heart.'* It was as if I grew to know in these deep moments that the Father was actively and relentlessly reaching out to me in my nightmare, in a real way like Ben Hur desperately searching for his mother and sister, searching even to the point of being consumed.

The critical difference of course was that the mother and sister of Ben Hur could not be aware of or be in touch with his love for them during the whole time of his relentless seach. But in my prayer and especially in moments of deep union after Eucharist, a growing intimacy with Jesus would render present this Love as a real experience. I began to know burning within the Love of a Father's Heart which could do nothing less than rush to me in my nightmare. A Presence beside me and walking with me unveiled for me to see and know *a Love in God for me.* It was a Love that would leave the ninety-nine sheep who were safe and enter gladly into an all-consuming search for my happiness.' It was a Love of God of such magnitude that it could make my healing and joy His whole occupation and relentless quest!

How did prayer yield to me such a conviction about the reality of this Love? How could I be so sure of my vision of this Love as something real, something touching the realm of fact and ?xperience? I can only respond by asking how one can really know a father's love, or a mother's love? How does a little girl engulfed in darkness find comfort and security in the certainty of a "father's" loving embrace? As "real presence" gave Claire this assurance, so also my conviction was born of "Real Presence." It could only be that His Presence came close to me in my prayer. Like a child, I became secure as His Presence enveloped me and embraced me. Like a child I knew security and peace, but only when real Presence came close enough in the moment of prayer, so close that I could search the eyes of God and see in them a Heart of divine Love that had been given to me.

*The Experience of Faith — the Vision of His
Divine Love Born of Prayer and Communion*

And so in the darkness of my nightmare and my prison, I found thrusting forth from my prayer the dawn of true Faith. In the light of that dawn there unfolded for me a clear vision, awareness, and experience of the Father's tender Love for me. My immediate task was only to hold fast to this experience of Faith, to this vision and experience of great Love despite the darkness that I saw. I began to understand in those dark moments of that November storm that in its essential definition the experience of Faith could be nothing less than *this vision and experience of infinite Love born of an intimate communion with God in prayer and Eucharist.*[5] This vision of Love, this experience of God born of prayer was in fact the heart of Faith and the goal of Faith. What was really happening in fact over the whole course of my trial was the birth of true Faith, Faith itself finding fulfillment and fruition, Faith as an experience of God's Love in Christ finally coming alive and becoming a reality for me. I had seen the experience of Faith in my little Claire deeply knowing the father's heart even in her nightmare. Faith was my little girl knowing her father's Love as a real experience even as she cried out in the darkness with outstretched arms and hands. Now Faith was me in the Ann Arbor "night'" always open, waiting, yielding, in surrender to my Father Whom I knew to be Love for me.

It was in prayer and the communion of Eucharist that I had come to the experience of this Presence in my heart upon which Faith thrives and builds. It was in the communion of prayer that I had come to Faith as a vision and experience of divine Love that is firm and real even in the moment of our darkest hour and trial. I found growing in my heart a Presence of strength and force. It was a strength and force making it possible for me not to believe the darkness that I could see surrounding me, but more and more to see even in the most fierce of storms what I as a Catholic had supposedly "believed," but not really: that God's Heart had been given to be and *pierced* for me, that He was Love for me.

My Faith then was now a sustained and growing experience of the Father's Love for me in communion with Christ, even in the darkest hour. And yet what I was still to find out was that given the fact of this Faith, a moment of power and healing would never be long to follow. I had still to learn the lesson of Jesus to Martha. Given that she believed, she would behold the power of God, the resurrection from the dead, the healing of disease, a new creation rising forth from me, from one as good as a corpse.

Chapter 4

An Interlude:
A Parallel Event In The Life
Of The Saint From Lourdes

A new life began for me in that November. It was a new life in the dawn of a great vision. I could now understand for the first time the power source for the strength of great Faith in the saints, for example of Bernadette Soubirous* long after her apparitions had ceased. It was born of prayer, and now like her, yes even like her, I too was knowing this growing vision of divine Love as a real experience. As with Bernadette, the strong embrace of God's Love growing in my heart was clearly experienced as a fact flowing forth from Prayer and Holy Communion.' As with saints who had always seemed so super-human, my eyes too could in fact gaze with love upon a Real Presence of my Father's Spirit, and that Real Presence could become the dream and goal of my life and heart.' As with Bernadette, I too could share the experience of a loving gaze upon my Father Who was now really present to me' as He was to her in the Spirit of Jesus and, if you will, in the Spirit of Mary** as well. For the first time in my life I could really believe that I too was beginning to experience in Christ the odyssey of Bernadette to this vision of the Father's Love, an odyssey to great Faith", and I was beginning to experience this

*An excellent source here is *St. Bernadette Soubirous* by Francis Trochu.
**Mary is the Mother of all who are alive with Christ's Love. If I am alive with His Love, my Life in a most real way has come forth from her. The Lord in His Joy has willed this for her — to be Mother of the Church alive with God's Fire.

within me precisely through a divine movement of the same Love which she knew, and which was now present in my own heart.

It was like unlocking a miraculous secret. I had always admired Bernadette from afar, as if her sanctity and the power of her Faith wwere beyond the realistic limits of human aspiration — with or without grace. She like all the saints had become like a legend grounded in unreality. After all, how could she face the ridicule of thousands of people while washing with water from a spring that did not exist? How could she not believe what the crowds so clearly saw? The spring did not exist. Yet she held fast to the word and vision of divine Love present in Mary, a word and vision that spoke of the spring's reality in spite of what she and the crowds could factually see.

Bernadette had the grace to hold fast a clear vision of divine Love, a vision which intimate prayer always kept alive and strong in her awareness even long after the power of apparitions ceased. Her strength to see born of prayer, her strength to gaze upon the Heart of God given up for her and pierced for her,' remained firm throughout her life, throughout a sea of storms. For the ridicule did not stop though the apparitions did. The suffering did not stop. The sacrifice and trial did not stop. Her sickness and infirmity only grew with intensity. Yet in the face of continually mounting adversity and personal disappointment, her faith, her vision and experience of God's Heart given to her and pierced for her remained undaunted.

Her sense of real communion with God present in prayer was firm and deep, undeniable and real, though there was little in her life to affirm her relentless insistence upon a gospel of God present to man out of total and infinite Love. "The spring was not for her." Healing was not for her. Wealth was not for her. The affirmation and elation of fame and praise were not for her. Only with her death would *the camouflage* and veil of this dark world be stripped away and the reality of God's Love become "all in all" for her, the reality of Lights as all-consuming and clearly seen as the noon-day sun. Yet until the end, Bernadette did not believe the darkness she saw engulfing her, as Mary at the foot of the cross did not believe the darkness she saw engulfing her. As Mary knew, she too knew that the promises made to her by the presence of God would be fulfilled, and she knew this precisely in the ex-

34

perience of Faith, in her moments of profound loving union with a Father'
Who was truly present and alive to her heart. In her prayer Truth
unfolded to her and embraced her. In Eucharist, as in prayer, Bernadette
knew that Jesus was present.[2]

And if darkness surrounded her, the Real Presence of Jesus within
was already a real Light and sign and pledge to her of a future promise
come true — the darkness, disease, and affliction could not last forever.
The true Light was already present and shining. Darkness could not last
forever. It was doomed to pass away.[3] Already it was robbed of its force
and sting.[4] Its time was short.[5] She had only to believe, to embrace her real
vision and experience of divine Love, even if for years, even if it should cost
her everything for this Love worth more than she could ever pay.[6] She had
only to hold fast to Faith, and she would behold the power of God' moving
her toward healing and perfection of body, mind, and Spirit.[8]

For wherever Jesus was present, power would have to flow forth
from Him[9] as a Light shattering darkness, disease, and the oppressive
weight of trial. Where the Light shines, the darkness cannot remain. Where
God is fully present the blind would have to receive their sight. The lame
would walk. Lepers would be cleansed and the deaf would begin to hear.
The dead would be raised up to life. Joy would have to transform the lives
of the poor.[10] God walking the earth is in fact the Presence of Power to
overcome the world.[11] The forces of death's realm cannot prevail against
God present in power as an opposing and greater force of Good.[12]

Chapter 5

The Reign Of The Spirit's Power

The Reign of the Spirit's Power; An Unchallenged Law
Governing The Experience of the Man Who Believes, Compelled
into Being by the Fact and Presence of the Fathers Love'

And so it was that like Bernadette, like Mary, like Martha at the tomb of Lazarus, I found a growing sense of strength issuing forth from my prayer in the "night."' It was a strength to face the day in the embrace of God's Love, and this strength grew with my increasing awareness and experience of that Love.

But there was still something seminal, seed-like, or primordial about my sense and awareness of this strength. The stench of the tomb still surrounded me. The darkness of Calvary still engulfed me. I was twenty-two at the time, but it still would have been difficult to convince me that my definitive' ;end and failure were not near at hand. As yet nothing had really changed for the better on the surface of my life. I still felt exhaustion, and a sense of being depleted and ineffective. The alarm reactions in my heart and lungs remained, and above all the tremor in my hands, the embarrassing tremor...

Yet in the face of all of this, my prayer had given me access to a strength that was real, and there was a growing awareness in my mind and heart • of this strength to deal with my life and my trials in the experience of Faith, the real experience of God's Love intimately present and so alive to me.' I grew strong in the intimate experience and reassuring Presence of Jesus

Who walked with me and revealed to me the Father's Love.¹ In the face of overwhelming darkness, my heart would burnt with a real strength and conviction and hope in the prayer of each night.

"Were our hearts not burning within us as He talked to us on the road, while He opened the Scriptures to us?"³ I too found myself on the road to Emmaus. Like the two disciples on that road, I too was at a point where hope was dead, all reason for Faith destroyed, the darkness definitive. But in the prayer of each night healing Presence and Peace without reason for being would stand by me, touch me, and walk with me.⁴ And like these two disciples, I too found myself each evening inspired and strengthened as Christ spoke. *His words* were already like the dawn of great Light unfolding to my view and vision. In the face of the tomb's stench and Good Friday's pain, there was already a security and strength as He held me and reassured me.

But like these same disciples there was a sense of something happening to me all too fast. You might say that like them, until a "moment of Communion" still to come, there was a "dawning"° sense and awareness of Power with me which even yet I would hardly dare to embrace. As with these disciples, I had only to believe, to embrace the fact of God with me despite the sense of night and emptiness and despair engulfing me that was all too real, but it was in my excitement more than I could grasp or hope for. Like them, I would have to see something. Yet like these disciples, I too was called and chosen precisely to behold the unchallenged power of God's Love in a moment of communion.° I was to see — I had only to believe,' to hold fast this vision of my evening prayer, the experience of God's Love for me walking by my side night by night in the Spirit of the Risen Christ.°

I was to see the unchallenged power of that Love as a healing power no less real and decisive in its force than the power present on the road to Emmaus or the road to Damascus⁹ or in the valley of Lourdes, the healing power of God's Love not only present to me," but infusing me, shattering my death with His Life, my trembling with His strength and with renewed zeal."

With explosive awareness generated from Broken Bread and a saving Cup" I too was called to see in a moment all too near that His Presence was not only Love but Power." I too was called to see that God could not be present to me but in power. His Presence was in substance the Presence of an unchallenged Force, of Love that could only transform) and raise to Life.'

An event, a happening, a moment of awakening about to unfold at the height of my Ann Arbor trial — I want so much to tell what it was, but even more to tell what it meant. It would *bring deeply into my awareness* the fact that God is *always* present precisely as an unchallenged Force of transforming Love.[3] In its Light I would realize the Power that is known intimately only by the child leaping into the embrace of a Father's Love.[4] I was that child. I was the son "leaping," the child now striving with the prayer of each night only to receive this Love and deepen my union with God's Presence.

My own life and experience would realize the Power in the Cross, what it was for Jesus Himself to be intimately guarded and enveloped by the force and strength of a Father's Love.' In my own life I was about to see as never before the reign of His Spirit's power as an immutable law and force, directing and governing every experience emerging in my life. I would come to see the reign of God's Love as a law, a must, a necessity compelled into being wherever God is present and one with the heart of man. More than ever before this reign of His Love was a law and necessity that had to unfold to my own experience precisely because I had opened to that Love. Even now I knew more than ever with the prayer of each night His Love as present to me and for me, as undeniably real and alive to my experience. Imminently I would know as well the power of that Love to transform me, the power of that Love as a decisive force in the face of all evil, even the full fury of Satan.

If then "the forces of death's realms" seemed at first to overwhelm me at this time in my life, this event all too near for joy would show me otherwise. It would show me that this assault of evil could only grow more impotent and ineffective before the increasing fact of a Father's unchallenged Love actively and imminently at work in my life. It would show me that the assault of night could only lose its sting and fury in the face of divine transforming Light,' a Light even before this moment growing more deeply present to me each day, becoming each day more intimately one with my own heart. This event all too near would reveal clearly and fully that even for me this assault of night and evil could only be precisely what it was for Jesus in the Passion — a deceit and camouflage trying to shroud from His view the reality of His Father's Love, a Love deeply and totally present in power as a transforming and unchallenged Force.

The event would generate in me a profound sense of gift,' the gift to see my life and especially my trial in a whole new way — in the experience of Faith, in the Light and Presence of Jesus, with Jesus, as a child of God intimately one with Jesus His Son.' With graphic and total awareness, my whole experience of the Father's Love growing daily with prayer was now to be a reality touching my life in Jesus, with Jesus, through Him; a reality touching my life in prayer attentive to His Word, in the communion of Eucharist, in the sacraments that would release to me His healing Presence. Intimately one with Jesus, I was to know His experience and enter into His experience. I was to enter His Life, the Life of the Son, and I was to see and know only with Him and in Him the constant reality and eternal fact of a Father's Love as a decisive power changing the course of my life. As with the disciples on the road to Emmaus, I was to see undeniably with Jesus and in Jesus the reality of the Father's Presence as an unchallenged Force of transforming Love always present and alive to the experience of men who believe. I was to see that Love present even in the hour of the Passion, even in this hour of my own passion, even in that hour when hope seems impossible and the darkness definitive and total.

My fear, my trembling, my weakness, the censure and ridicule of the world, the fury of "night" were still there. But in the fact of this moment to come, they could not prevail before the deepening sense of Life, Light, and strength born in the embrace of a Father's Love and never before more alive and real to my experience.

A moment then was imminently to dawn upon me, a moment of communion where I was to become vividly conscious of what I would call the unchallenged reign of the Spirit's power. I was to see His Light present as a decisive and an unchallenged Force of transforming Love. I was to see that the Light is not just Presence, but Power in the face of night. As darkness cannot live in the Light, despair, evil, sin cannot live in His Presence. It was only a question of union, of entering into His Presence and Light, of entering into Him.' That done to any degree and then where the Light of God's Love is present, I would have to speak of Power truly present as well, Power that can vanquish the darkness and overcome the full fury of evil. I would have to speak of an experience of Presence that is also the Power of God's Spirit within me, the Spirit of a Father's Love reigning unchallenged over all other forces. I would have to speak of a Father's Love present to me in His Spirit that is in substance an unchallenged Force guiding and directing all the events of my life toward a critical end and goal. And that end and goal and dream of this Father's Love is nothing less than my freedom, healing, Life, and strength, born and flowing forth from an ever-deepening union with His own Presence.

"Seek first the Kingdom of God, and all these other things shall be yours as well."' I had only to seek the reign of His Spirit, my heart and mind consumed with the Love that is His Spirit and my own healing, freedom, and rejuvenation would not be long to follow. But how clear it would become that they were the fruit and effect of a union with God that was the deeper reality something more pivotal, essential, foundational, something at the center of life's meaning.

This moment to come, all too near for joy, would reveal so much to me — but mainly this union with God's Presence as the key to my own healing and rejuvenation. I was to see that I had really only one task in life that was truly needful — union with God in the Spirit of Christ," and in this union to see and know always with Jesus and in Jesus the growing vision of my evening prayer, the real vision and experience of His Father's Love transforming Power. Yet the transformation was to be effect and fruit. The root and cause, the Vine and Life was to be oneness with the Father's Love. *His Father's Love present to me* and one with me *was to be everything* for me." He was far more than just my healing and strength, far more than all I could ask or imagine."

Given this union I was to know with striking force as never before that I had now only to believe and nothing could hurt me." I had only to embrace and hold fast this vision of Him, and I could reject as hollow what I see and hear in the night. I could disbelieve the lie, the camouflage, and the deceit of the night." Now and for the rest of my days on earth, I had power in

40

this intimacy, embrace, and union, to "curse" and resist the voice of night and her children — the voices of fear, worry, weakness, and despair; voices thriving in the darkness and turbulence that always threaten to engulf our lives.

And so a moment was imminently to dawn upon me, a moment of communion that would teach me clearly that God could not be present within me but as transforming Power. It is a Power that strives with all the force of God's Spirit to touch the man who believes with an ever-deepening experience of the Father's Love.' In this moment soon to come, His Presence would become such Power released into my life and experience that I could look with hope beyond the crucifixion, beyond my tragic defeat, beyond the tomb. His Presence would become a Power of Light, healing, deliverance, streaming forth to pierce the night and declare the darkness a lie and a fraud. In this moment soon to come, the whole experience of my own resurrection would dawn upon me and begin to assume a striking reality in my own awareness.

In fact, this entire event I was about to experience remains for me to this day the story of my own resurrection to life. It remains therefore a theophany of paramount importance for my life - what the Exodus was for the Hebrew people and precisely what the resurrection of Jesus was for Mary our Mother, for the saints, for all the disciples like myself called to walk with the Lord on the road to Emmaus.' What I was to experience has become in fact the central event of my lfie, teaching me to this day the meaning, essence, and substance of the Son's Faith in the loving care of His Father. There is a true sense in which I must date my conversion from the time of this event, for until now the Force of Jesus' Love was not Lord of my life and I was not yet free.

Chapter 6

The Embrace Of A Father's Love'

It was late on one November evening ten years ago that I made a special plea to God and His saints, to Mary and the child of Lourdes. It was a prayer made in a deep awareness of my Father's Love, an experience of Love generated in many intimate moments with Jesus and in Jesus. Those moments always grew to be more and more strong and consoling. They had become, with ever deepening force, a refuge for me. They had become a deep source of Light that stayed with me throughout my day, and with the prayer of each night that Light would strengthen and intensify. It was late one night toward the end of evening prayer that I made my special plea. I took water from Lourdes, from the Spring that "did not exist" and poured it over trembling hands and wrists that had become a symbol to me.

I cannot begin to express in fact what a powerful symbol this whole ritual was for me. There was a deep meditation going on, with a sense in prayer of strength and trust growing from the fact and experience of a Father's Love for me. Each day the world, my fear, and my weakness would tell me, as it had told Bernadette long ago, that there was no healing Spring, that there was no healing Love. Hope was impossible, and I reached for dreams beyond my grasp.

However, each night in prayer I became in my heart the child of Lourdes and the man of Faith. I became a man experiencing Presence, drinking from a healing Spring which the world could neither see nor know, knowing a transforming Peace the world could neither find, give, understand, or take from me.'

Bernadette totally rapt in a vision of divine Love had turned to drink from waters of life and healing which the crowds of thousands could not see. Now in the intimacy of prayer I looked beyond what the world could see. I became a child returning the tight embrace of my Father, running only to him as to my refuge and haven in the storm.' Without realizing it too deeply I was even now being moved to see that only God could be my Peace,' Happiness,' Healing,' Strengths and Joy.'

Upon pouring the water, I immediately felt a tingling sensation of heat emanating from my wrists. What I had undertaken as symbol was becoming reality before my eyes. It was as if I had been content merely to draw a picture or engage in vivid mediation, yet only to find that the picture had become alive. It was as if I had been content to mold a wood statue only to find that it had become flesh. But if I could communicate what was most deeply moving about this event, it would be the transformations in my spirit that accompanied this physical sensation.

There was simultaneously a "baptism," a sense of being immersed, consumed and overwhelmed by the Power of the Father's Spirit." I was overwhelmed by the Force which is God's Love, and this is a degree unlike anything I could ever have imagined possible. It was in this moment that something critical dawned on me that was to radically change the course of my life.

Basically on that night I came to realize and experience what I had always given credence to as a Christian, yet without fire, life, or enthusiasm. I had believed it as part of a multitude of people do today by honoring God with their lips while their hearts are far from Him." What I came to realize was precisely that in this moment I was touching my Dream," my Quest my God, the true Goal of all my life's aspirations and noble ambitions." In the overwhelming experience of the Power of His Love truly present to me, I had definitively come to a moment in the Presence and embrace of my Father where I could really say I "...have nowhere else to go."' Let me pitch a tent and remain and not move from this moment." I could so clearly experience and see the Spirit of total Love for me. It was as if in the Power taking hold of me, in the Father embracing me, I had come close enough to see the delight in His face for me. I had come close enough to feel the heart of God

43

pulsating with pride over the beauty of His son.

I cannot begin to tell you how I was now drawn and anointed to be intimate, one, and happy with God my Father' as a focus for the effort and striving of my whole life. That was the miracle, the critical change of course, the healing in the core of my spirit that would ultimately and did ultimately effect my physical healing as well. The years to come saw in fact the termination of my alarm reactions and even more importantly, the rejuvenation of my energy to love with zeal and joy and fire.'

From that moment each day of my life would be an effort and quest to come and put myself through prayer and Eucharist in the presence of God, a God Who was waiting with expectant longing' all the years of my life and of time itself for me to come to Him for Life.· *He* wanted to be the substance and essence of my dreams — not peace or happiness or healing. They were to be the fruit and effect of a deeper Quest, a deeper Reality.' And He was that Reality. He wanted me to find my fulfillment, my healing, my food' in Him, in the embrace of my Father's Love.

A seed of new life was planted in that moment. It was the beginning of a radical change in the direction and focus of my life. I could no longer describe my life quest as the dream of being the purest and highest embodiment of an Ann Arbor Apostle, a powerful, persuasive preacher, an effective evangelist. I was now filled with a thirst for God.' From this time, at the heart of my purpose in life, there was to be this movement within me drawing me irresistibly' to know God with the intimacy of a "Son" enveloped by a Father's Love. I was drawn to know God with the intimacy of a spouse who knows in the joy of intercourse that the Bridgroom is Love for her.' *The crux of my disease prior to that night and a disease rampantly infecting others of the Church of our time, was this basic disorder in the focus of my life and heart.'°*

Chapter 7

The End Of Man And The Way To Joy

A Ceaseless Striving to Know God as the
Son Knows the Father in Love

In the prayer of that November night I began to experience the power of the Father's Love 'effecting within me an authentic transformation.' That Love so fully alive and present was radically altering the focus of my life and heart. God Himself was to become my focus. I was overwhelmed and drawn to seek Him by an irresistible movement of Presence within. As a Catholic I could always understand this focus conceptually. I could even want it, but only as the dreams of my youth would reach in futility for the Love of the Saints. *Only now in this experience of Faith did I know Power to relinquish every other ambition and move home' toward my Father as a focus for the effort and striving of my whole life.*

My experience was like that which many of us have had or will have at some time or other. We know that if only we'd give ourselves a break, a chance to get away, a leave of absence, a vacation for time to see our wife, our close friends, our loved ones, then we would move easily toward healing and rejuvenation. We would find rest from the turbulence and anxiety of life. But we don't. There are commitments. We are deeply engaged in so many "matters of consequence," and there is no energy, drive, or freedom to go home.

Until that night in November that was my experience of Life —

45

the anxiety — ridden behavior of the 20th century man. I knew at the deepest level of the heart was my need for God, and my need for Him in a real sense as "Home," or as the healing, restoring Love that only "Home" can give. This need was as absolute as a child's need for the parent's love. It was as absolute as Man's need for food, water, sun, and the air he breathes. But there was no energy, drive, or freedom to go "Home"' within me. The whole movement of my life was taking me further and further away from "Home," and I could not stop it. If I were ever to get "Home", a Power, a strength,' and a drive beyond what I knew within myself would have to get me there. I was not free. "The good I wanted to do, I did not, and the evil I wanted to avoid, that I found myself doing..."'

With critical urgency it dawned on me in the prayer of that night that I *needed* to accept an offer of God's Love and Power. I needed to yield in loving openness to this Spirit of my Father. I needed this as much as I needed to receive food.' And food is a good image here because there is in natural life a sense of growth, transformation, a coming to strength or healing of weakness, a coming to fullness of health and Life itself *only through food.* I had only to seek food, to *focus* on food, and all these other realities such as growth, strength, and healing would be mine as well - in a real sense, I didn't even have to worry about them or even think about them, only about food.'

My sense of the critical need for the Father's Loves and Presence dawned on me in exactly this same light. They were Food for me. I had only to focus on them, seek them, direct my concern only to them. Without this Food that is the Father's Love, there is no coming to strength or healing of weakness.' Unless we receive and embrace His Love for us, there is no transformation,' no coming to a fullness of health and Life itself. Every effort of mine to be a Christian, to live a life for God would become in fact a masquerade, a folly, a sham as doomed to defeat and death as an infant cast out into the cold, or more pointedly, as ludicrous as a marriage with only one Spouse.' *It struck me that night in the core of my being that by my very nature I am incomplete of myself, unfulfilled of myself.*° Like the infant I needed Someone to "draw"'' me "Home," to take me "Home," I needed to become like a little child." I needed to become born again."

46

I came to realize with deep feeling that as a Christian and even as a man, simply by the fact that I am a human being, this crucial insight articulated a fundamental need that cries out from the very depths of what I am. Through my birth into this world I am by my very nature a bride placed in a "wedding chamber" totally helpless for *my joy and fulfillment* until *Christ the Bridegroom becomes that for me.'* I lay lifeless, inanimate, and uninspired until the Bridegroom enters the room and reveals to me in the joy of intercourse that He completes me. It is He that is Love for me,² and in His Love it is He that longs to complete me. And there is a strength, an energy, a healing and "food," a fulfillment and completion which cannot be mine as long as I decide to reject Christian Faith' — to remain in my isolation, alone and unloved, courting the delusion that I am self-subsistent.

The Contemporary Folly
This delusion⁴ is the contemporary folly — the 20th century man who is really a child without Faith, an infant deciding for his independence of a "Parent's Love." It is a folly which explains for me the lethal striving of so many 20th century men — their relentless working, doing, performing and achieving to the point where they deliberately sacrifice prayer, evenings at home, time with spouse and children, and the pursuit of friendship.⁵ It is a movement and striving that I too was caught up in. The whole movement of my life that was taking me further and further away from "Home," taking me further and further from the Father's Love.

And really, why this desolate movement, why this deadly striving? At the heart of it, why? I think that at the roots of this whole phenomenon, *we're dealing with the proud effort of contemporary man to consolidate his own independence by finding a substitute for what only divine Love can give us.⁶* I would cling to this insight. I would challenge every other insight I have before comprising it. The delusion and disguise takes the form of many motives, but for a multitude of people today, behind this disguise, behind this relentless work and ceaseless striving to "make it in the business world" or "climb the corporate ladder," there is an insatiable need to be loved that only God can satisfy. Behind this relentless work and ceaseless striving to rise to fame at the summits of worldly or secular success, behind this ceaseless striving to get the Ph.D. even at the cost of health and family, or to write that book that will get us on "Mike Douglas," radio, or "The Johnny Carson Show" — yes, behind this disguise is an insatiable need to be loved that only God can satisfy. It is a fundamental need that was given man from the origins of time when he came forth in a creative act, born of Love from the heart of the Father.' All this work toward the attainment of public attention, recognition, world renown, toward the attainment of some sense of worth and importance — completion if you will — is in fact pride's futile and desperate effort to find what only the embrace of the Father's Love can give.

What I see behind today's idolatry of work, the effort of work to baptize a ruthless quest for success and the fame it will bring, is nothing less than the height of madness. It is the folly of human affairs steeped in pride. It is the tragedy of an infant striving insanely for independence of a "Parent's care."ₗ What I discern is the folly of a bride choosing isolation in her wedding chamber, locking the door to any advance of a loving Spouse. For me it was in Ann Arbor that the impact of this truth dawned to my awareness and spoke to the heart of my own problem — what am I as man, and what is the reason, definition, and the very nature of this created existence which I enjoy? Man is a spouse invited by his birth to enter a Divine Wedding. He is the infant crying out by definition for the absolute need which is a Parent's Love.ᴊ It was in my Ann Arbor experience that I saw this for the first time, and I saw too the unnerving ramifications, had I refused the advance of a Spouse's Love and a Father's care...

Truth of Crucial Impact for the Whole Church
Of course, implied in all of this was an awareness that these truths were at the heart of "being a Christian" — they were truths not just for me, but for the whole Church. At the heart of a "life for God" had to be this identification and oneness with Jesus as the "Son"ₛ — with Jesus as One Who is "of God," as One born of the "Father"ₜ and drawing life from Him.'

Now conceptually I knew all along as a Catholic that the Church was supposed to be the Body of Jesus,ᴊ the only "Son" of the "Father" living on in the world of our own day and time. Concept-

48

tually I knew that the Church, if ever to be dynamic and alive, had to be in its substance and definition like Jesus, the child running to the outstretched hands of a Loving Father as to His meat and food.' And I "knew" that I too was part of the Church.

Yet until this moment in Ann Arbor there was never any impact and power in my contemplation of any of these truths. I "knew", them, but not really. I began to realize that as part of the Church, what Faith in Christ had called me to see and what I needed to believe was precisely what the infant believes about the parent's care and the spouse about the loving advance of the Bridegroom. My baptism, my pursuit of Holy Communion, my involvement in the Body of Christ on earth — all these really called me to acknowledge a fundamental fact: that I was created to need the Father's care for my completion and fulfillment.

I had to become like my little Claire calling out to "Daddy" in her nightmare. I had to become like a child crying out in the "night,", focusing on my Father and guarding my heart for the Light' that only He could be for me. Only in His embrace would I find fulfillment, completion, my strength, my healing, and my food. As part of the Church, as part of the Body of Christ on earth today, my fulfillment was precisely in this call to become as Jesus "going to the Father,", to become as the Son moving Home toward my Father as a focus for the effort and striving of my whole life. This movement had to become my essential definition, what I was all about at the very core of my being. This movement had to become my dream,' my life's quest and ambition. *And I realized that unless there would now be a ceaseless striving to seek the goal and focus that was my Father, I would be courting an essentially faulty and defective idea of what it is to be a Christian. I would be courting a defective idea of what it is to live wholeheartedly for God.*

Precisely because I was part of the Church, because I was decidedly a part of the Body of Christ upon earth, my life was called to witness to and attest to a fundamental imperative, an essential truth: that like Jesus the "Son,", the man Who is "of God" and really a child "of the Father," looks to a Food outside of himself for the power of Life and Love and Goodness.' Even my acceptance of the sacraments had to mean an attempt on my part to say that God was my Strength and Food. For what else is

Mass if not that event each day where I enter into the Life of the Son and become myself a "son" in the embrace of Power, a bride wedded to a transforming Fire' that I would never know in isolation, alone and unloved, left to myself, to my own ceaseless effort and striving?

Truth of Critical Impact for All Men

Yet in the light of all this reflection, I must underscore that I cannot only see my witness to these insights as simply for Catholicism or for the Christian Church, but for all men. I say this because it is as a man that I cry out for completion in God. It is perhaps this realization which would best represent the height and climax of what I began to see in the Ann Arbor experience. I began to realize that all of the crucial insights born of this experience directed their gaze not just toward me or even just toward the Christian Church called by its very nature to sublime identity and oneness with the only "Son" "of the Father." These insights were truth of critical impact whose sweeping gaze was meant to encompass all men. The truth of these words spoke with striking, piercing light concerning the end of all men and of their way to joy — that the end and joy of all men as well as myself, was a ceaseless striving to know God as Jesus the Son knows the Father in Love.

And there is a supreme height of folly to 20th century human affairs only because men do not embrace this fundamental truth. They deny it. They refuse to discern and understand our essential nature as men born for God. "Our hearts are made for you, 0 God, and we cannot rest until we rest in you."* Where today in our world is any semblance of a belief thrusting forth from our deeds and speech that God is our Rest, the Meat and Food nurturing our sense of fulfillment? Where is there any striking conviction that God's Love is the fuel giving fire to the j oy of our existence? There are indisputable *signs* of an absolute need for His Love, but where is there any conviction that man is the spouse invited by his birthday to enter a Divine Wedding? Where is there any conviction that he is the infant son crying out for the Father's Love?

Did I believe this? Not really. I was a product of my world and American culture, the bridegroom of Pride drowning in my delusion of independence

*This thought is from the *Confessions of St. Augustine.*

50

along with most of my contemporaries. My life gave every indication that we cannot become complete, fulfilled, and whole, but from the Love of the Bridegroom. Every effort to deny my total dependence upon the Father's Love did not render that Love any less needed, and needed absolutely.'

But in this denial of which I too was guilty rests the supreme folly of the current day. The denial is subtle, yet real and all- pervasive. In fact, contemporary men choose to build their lives on a lie.₂ They deny their basic and absolute need for God's Love and for the completion and fulfillment they find only in His embrace. They spurn the invitation to enter a Divine Wedding, and then begins the *amazing* paradox. Avoiding Love, they search for what Love alone can give. They begin a desperate search and relentless striving for a sense of worth, importance, completion, and wholeness which can be ours only through the gift of a Father's embrace — and this known as a real fact in the experience of His Spirit.₃

I think that there is overwhelming support for these conclusions in the current widespread phenomenon of people facing life alone, in isolation, in fact divorced from God or any real intimacy with Him. You might say in the lives of so many people today, I fail to discern any sense of God intimately present and known as a real Spouse. What I'm talking about becomes clear when we look at the real parallel today in so many empty, hollow marriages where one spouse seems in fact to be such a distant and irrelevant concern to the heart of the other. And it doesn't even matter whether such people are married lawfully. In fact, their marriage seems to be only that and nothing wore — marriage "on paper" or according to law — for really, the marriage doesn't make any difference in their lives.₄ It changes nothing for them. Even long after marriage, an attitude seems to linger on as if deeply entrenched: "I still don't need anyone or any help."

These marriages are a masquerade and mockery of any real "union in Love," and this is the critical point which parallels what I would want to observe about the similar "union with God in Love" of a multitude of people today, even that of many "Christian" people.' Supposedly by our Baptism we lawfully enter a Divine Wedding;' we are called to embrace God in the intimacy of a Spouse, but what real difference today does

51

Baptism make *in* fact. I fail to discern everywhere today, in the world, but also in the Church, anything beyond "lip service"[1] to the real call at the heart of Christianity. I fail to discern any real sense of living intimately with Someone, any authentic sense of making decisions and facing the challenges of life with Someone closely by my side ready to comfort and strengthen me. I fail to discern any sense of even being open to this experience, of being open to this experience at the heart of Christian Faith.

On the contrary, man today strengthens his isolation through wealth, and out of fear of losing that wealth man becomes deaf and cold to the need of others, thus compelling their aloneness as well as his own. Then in isolation man pursues the folly, the amazing paradox, or perhaps better stated, the endless, vicious cycle leading only to deeper need and deeper starvation. He pursues food, but avoids Food. He avoids Love but seeks what only Love can give. He will work 78 to 90 hours a week, at times even demanding isolation in his own home, toward the end of earning from an employer and colleagues some sense of recognition, a sense of worth and importance he would readily receive from his friends, his spouse, and his God. But he has no time to see them and to be embraced by them. The whole movement of his life takes him further and further away from their healing Love, further away from "Home."

To First Touch the End of Man and the Way to Joy in the Prayer of One November Night

I was part of this. In my case there was an attempt to spend relentless hours laboring, achieving, doing the work of an apostle, preacher, and evangelist — all in the hope of receiving the warmth of Love, even from God's people, but only on the terms of pride: in the form of recognition, reputation for excellence, prestige, success. At the heart of my problem was a person feeling unloved, unaffirmed, unappreciated, and simultaneously a person directly attaching no time and no importance to moments of loving union with God or His people.

But you can't pursue food and yet avoid Food. Only Food can be Food. Only God could be God for me. All else proved hollow and empty. I still was always thirsty. Endless labor could not purchase the deep sense of worth that one moment of the Father's

52

embrace would give as a free gift.' If there had only been frequent moments of loving union with the Lord and His people — and that seen as the goal of my whole life and work — I would have ceased being "busy" to the extent that I was. I was doing a great amount of empty work — work that was all for the sense of self-worth and affirmation which work could never really give. Work would then have ceased being an obsession and oppression for me. If I had had the knowledge that I was deeply loved and not alone, the need for endless hours of vain labor would have ceased. I needed only to forsake my isolation and unlock the door to my wedding chamber, to unlock my heart to God's embrace and respond to Him in love; I needed only to pray, to enter Christ!

In our current-day culture though, this seemed almost a forbidden course of action, and to this day I am under pressure not to take it. But in the prayer of one November night I recognized the supreme folly for what it is. No longer is my life my quest alone. It is no longer my quest but "ours" — the quest of God with me. It is no longer my dream' I pursue, but His dream as well. From that time I have rejected the folly of isolation and the world endorsing it. I have rejected this "West World"* that settles for a hollow and lifeless fabrication, a clone, a mechanical double. It is the world that settles for the lunacy of embracing chains in the pursuit of freedom; of embracing isolation behind locked doors, yet all in the pursuit of love. "The wisdom of this world is foolishness with God." I reject the madness of this vain world, a world which carefully plots a collision course with God, by a futile effort to take Him with it along a tragic path of pride.

*Allusion here to a recent film with this title.

Summation

The Ann Arbor Experience
As The Experience Of Faith

My life experienced a critical change of course in the prayer and power of "one Ann Arbor night.'" As a sense of heat burned in my wrists, a sense of piercing Light and Powers seized my spirit and captured my will. It was the first time in my life where I could clearly know, as a real experience, the Loves and Power of the Father's Spirit taking hold of me and radically altering the focus of my life and heart.

From that moment on, my experience of Christianity would be an experience of freedom,° the experience at the heart of Christian Faith. The years yet to unfold would be an unhindered movement toward "Home,'" toward my Father, toward Him as toward a Focus for the effort and striving of my whole life. The power of His embrace raising me to freedom') had become a vibrant reality, not lifeless words to which I gave the honor of lip service,° while never feeling the impact of their truth. From that moment I knew" the Love of my Father. From the moment I would speak of what I knew and bear witness to what I had seen.

In those late hours of "one Ann Arbor night" I was once again a little boy with my father, racing around my neighborhood block. His Love embracing me was everything. I was free of all anxiety in the overwhelming experience of His Love.'' The vision of His divine Love for me, His son, consumed the whole of my attention. I could focus on nothing less than this fact of His total Love. In the joy of this piercing Light, my heart became blind to all other care.

It was the first time that I knew and felt what I would come to know more deeply in all the dark hours' of my life. I was in the arms of an all-powerful Love, rendering me secure and at peace when the world could give me no reason for peace. There was a sense of being caught up and rapt in joy, of being apprehended by my Father. He was reaching out to His son enveloped and tormented by a nightmarish vision. Divine transcendent power surged into me, His earthen vessel, and through the freedom born of His power I found myself moving Home toward my Father as toward a Dreams and Goal for the effort and striving of my whole life.

In this grace-given moment He had become my thirst and I was being drawn irresistibly to know Him. I was being drawn to God away from the world, but unlike I had always believed, there was no sense of renouncing the world in the pain of great and arduous sacrifice. I could only feel so deeply the joy of Francis and all the saints in being released from the world as from a great burden, as if chains holding me back had been snapped and broken by an incredible Force.' Now I was lost to the world in the joy of an intercourse far beyond all I could ask or imagine!'

To the vision of the world I had nothing, but in truth I possessed everything, I was engrossed and absorbed in the vision of a Love," of a Lover, Whom the world cannot see, " while the earthly sight of what can be seen proved hollow, empty, unreality and a lie." I wanted only this Love, the experience of this Love, really, the experience of Christian Faith." I wanted only to become this Love for a diseased world drowning in its pride and folly. To be such healing Love would become my dream. To lead others to such Love would become my dream as well, for I could not but think that Love would have it so. This quest for His Love would be my dream, my charismatic dream, but a dream that was the Father's dream as well, His dream for the Christian Church and the whole of mankind."

PART III

The deeper problem:
To proclaim words that lead to power

Chapter 1

The Powerful Experience
That Is Christian Faith

To Enter into the Life of Jesus, the Son,
As He Lives, Moves, and Has His Being
in the Embrace of His Father's Love

How does someone go about presenting Christian Faith? Why would one sense a need to present a more clear idea of what Christian Faith is and what it involves?

In the recent past large portions of the "Christian population" in the West have taken Christian Faith, the most powerful phenomenon to ever penetrate human existence, and have reduced it to something impotent, sterile, and lifeless. They have reduced it to something gaunt — something that is only a pale and emaciated shadow of its former self. They have reduced it to something we see rampant today; the sublime folly of a Christianity and Christian Faith where "Christians" do not even know if God is real; where "Christians" discard the question of God's existence as irrelevant at best and open themselves only to some amorphous ideals of "Love," "Brotherhood," and "Peace," which they naively place within the powers of their own attainment.

The height of this sublime folly and masquerade of Christianity is the "polite" attempt to make Jesus some sort of occasional and incidental "allusion," "a source" if you will for our grandiose ideals, but only one along with a host of other great men from history. The height of this sublime masquerade of Christian Faith is the contemporary attempt to assign Jesus some outlandish role as merely a great moral teacher who is inscrutable and beyond knowing behind the barrier of ancient times. The epitome of this masquerade is the contemporary attempt to prohibit and preclude anything but this Jesus Who remains inscrutable and beyond knowing, swallowed up in the secret and mystery of an age and moment long ago, forever lost to our vision and experience.

In the light of this situation, one with any substantial biblical idea of what Christian Faith is all about, can only say that this is a most abhorrent and pitiable state of affairs. However, I think we can find the key to understanding how this disaster came about and have the key to its own correction when we enter into the experience of Jesus — in particular, an attempt simply to enter His own experience as "Son," and His own experience of God as "Father."[1]

Now in saying this it is not denied that to enter into and know this experience of Jesus as Son is of paramount importance for anyone at any time. I only intend to underscore the crucial value this effort holds for us if we would provide for ourselves an essential key to understanding the "disaster" infecting the Christianity of our day[2] — even more than this, an essential key toward the solution of any human problem and a crucial clue toward the cure of all the depression and unhappiness that afflict contemporary men.

This is a contention, or should I say "a boast," that sets up a tremendous expectation. However, there is much to gain for the simple price of entering into and knowing as my own the experience of Jesus as "Son," and His experience of God as "Father." In many ways it is like a "voice crying out in the wilderness."[3] "Come and see Light' where perhaps you never thought to look for light." "Come and touch Fire' where perhaps you never thought to find it before." And speaking from within an experience of Light and Fire that is nothing less than consuming, I can say with all the conviction that a man can summon to the support of reason; what we need to do in Christianity today is precisely to enter into and know as our own that real human experience of Jesus as Son which is the epitome of Christian Faith.'

58

To enter into this experience and to know it as our own is to know the experience of Christian Faith in all of its fullness, dynamism, and fire. It is really an effort to place within our grasp, not only the key to understanding the "disaster" which infects the Christianity of our own day, but as well the key and clue toward the solution of any human problem and any unhappiness which afflict, oppress, and dehumanize contemporary men.

Perhaps to state the case another way, I can say that to know this experience of Jesus as my own, to make His Life my own life,' to make it my goal and substance,; the dream at the heart of my day,; in a real sense the God of my existence, is really an effort to touch the power and force of basic Christianity.. To enter into and to know as my own this experience of Jesus as Son of the Father, is authentically an effort to touch the power and force, even the core and essential fabric of basic Christianity.'

This can be said* because basic Christianity is precisely what we are talking about when we speak of entering into the Life and experience of Jesus as Son, and of knowing in Him His own experience of God as Father.' What we are in fact talking about here is the essential experience of basic Christianity or basic Christian Faith.

Because this experience is missing, there is a force and power inherent in basic Christianity that is foreign and missing in today's Churches. An image that would be most effective here, would be to imagine how one could really understand the full meaning and power of "Mother" without an experience of the same. Would anyone even try! In the same vein how could anyone really understand the meaning and power of "Love" without an experience of the same. It is exactly as problematic to understand Christian Faith in the absence of an experience of Jesus because Christian Faith is essentially an experience of Jesus as much as "Mother" or "Love" has to be essentially an experience before I can know them and feel what they are.' Christian Faith too is, essentially an experience of Jesus — that is it has to be as "Love" is, an experience entered into and known personally before it can

*The power and force of Christianity achieves identity with it. This is not at all irregular or out of the ordinary. For example, the substance of baseball is a bat, a glove, and a ball. Baseball is more than these, but what is left to baseball without them? So also, flying is more than wings; love-making is more than sexuality, but what is left to flying without wings, or to love-making without sexuality? What is left to Christianity without its power and force — the Life and experience of Jesus?

be understood in all the fullness of its meaning and power.' For this very reason, to Paul, the Apostles, the Saints, the ancient Church, the very idea would seem absurd of trying to understand Christian Faith apart from the experience of Jesus!

Look at the following formulation of basic Christianity: union with the Father in Christ His Son Who lives and reigns within us and among us in the Person of God's Love, the Holy Spirit. For so many today this formulation reads and writes as boring, empty, lifeless words.

Yet Christian Faith need not be a string of boring, empty, lifeless jargon. It need not be just another dogmatic Church formulation which constitutes for so many today nothing more than abstract irrelevance or glorified nonsense. The formulation tragically amounts to this only because so many fail to touch the experience of Jesus, fail that is to enter into His experience and know it as their own, and without this experience they lose an essential ingredient toward any full understanding of the real meaning and power of basic Christianity. Could the word "Mother" or "Love" ever prove so boring, so lifeless — no, for we would never think to understand them apart from the experience of their reality so essential to any authentic grasp of their full meaning and power. But for Paul, the Saints and the Apostolic Church, to understand Christian Faith without the experience of Jesus would have seemed just as absurd, the epitome of folly.

My essential effort then would be to present the experience of Jesus as Son of the Father toward a more central effort to present basic Christian Faith and the power that is intrinsic to it. It might be said that at the heart of this writing there is critically an attempt to let basic Christianity emerge in all of its dynamism and force. This is precisely what happens when we begin to see the core and essential content of Christian Faith as an experience of Jesus. A *living experience of union* with the Father in Christ His Son remains for all time the essential and imperative ideal of Christian Faith. Yet this basic Christian Faith has a power inherently a part of it that is being missed by masses of people in contemporary Christian Churches. A real experience of Jesus essential to this ideal and any authentic understanding of it is absent, missing, foreign to contemporary men.

This situation initiates my reason for writing, for what could be more tragic than the experience of Jesus not present among us as the core reality and force of Christianity.' That this experience should be foreign to the men of today and even to Christians is more than unfortunate or tragic; it is destructive to the very existence of the Church and destructive to the very possibility of peace, unity, and brotherhood among all peoples.'

Yet the height of the tragedy is not that this experience of Jesus is missing today, but that it is not the central fact and experience especially in Christian Churches.' This experience of Christ at the heart of basic Christianity should not only be present and zealously proclaimed, but more so it should be the heart of the reason for the very existence of Christian Churches. Until this is evident there is the serious question as to why these Churches are even "in business." Now the Church is not a business any more than a family is a business, but this analogy to a business, though unseemly, is nevertheless pointed and highly instructive particularly in our own time. For it would seem that by and large many Christian Churches today are making the same mistake-and falling prey to the same malaise and delusion as are many contemporary businesses throughout our country.

Not to focus on social commentary, but there is a parallel and analogy here that is too plain and forceful to ignore. Many today, perhaps too much of a conservative school that is far from outdated, insist strongly that the profit will follow if only American enterprise would make a good product, whether car, food, or cup of coffee, instead of some plastic or synthetic substitute. Business' should not be first out to make a profit, but they should be first out to make a product — a high quality product. Make a needed, high quality product and the profit will come.

But so too with many Christian Churches today... We are not like a business out to make a profit, but like a business out to proclaim a product — in this case the experience of Christ and His Love. If we do our job and make Christ known, if we offer an experience of His Love, if we offer Christian Faith, "profit" will come in every sense of that word. But what will it "profit" us at all to gain the whole world and forfeit the Life that is ours only in the experience that is Jesus Christ and the Spirit of His Love?'

It is this experience alone which can tell us with force the crucial fact that we can know God as more real than we are to each other."

61

It is this experience alone which can "show us the Father,"[1] authentically present to us as a transforming energy of Love that is Christ's Spirit.[2] It is this experience alone which can tell us not only that "God is," "out there" somewhere, but that He wants to intervene decisively in our lives in that same reality of Christ's Spirit.[3]

This experience is then the explosive content and core of the Christian gospel and of Christian Faith. It was never the intent of Paul, the Saints, or the early Church to offer anything less than this experience, nor should it be the intent and tragic mistake of the Church in our own day. Yet in truth, unless this experience of Jesus is essential and imperative to the content and core of Christian Faith, we do in fact alienate ourselves from Paul, the Saints, and the Church of the Apostolic age; for we abandon a Faith which for all time must rest not on the wisdom of men and the prowess of intellectual systems, but on the power of God.[4]

Chapter 2

To Communicate An Experience Of God

How through words does one communicate the experience of Jesus that is Christian Faith?" How through words and writing could one even come to any "sense" of what this experience is? How through words and writing could one ever come to sense and feel what it is to believe, to enter into the real experience of Christ that is the vital nerve and crucial core of Christian Faith? How through words does one render present an experience of God, an experience of His Person? How - through words can one communicate an experience of His transforming Love? How through words do we render present an experience of Jesus, so that men might touch the power of that experience, and even more importantly, so that they might enter into His Life and make the experience of Jesus something they know as their own.

To state the problem in another way, if Christian Faith is an entering into Christ and becoming one with His Person, how in fact do we become one with a Person if He isn't real, and how through words do I pretend to make Him real? How through words do we go beyond analogies and metaphor, and arrive at a real experience of God present in power as a Love Who transforms me, heals me, and gives me as grace the courage to be free? I have only words to work with and yet how through words do I make it possible for someone to join himself to a real experience of Jesus Christ, so that the reality and not the myth of a Father's Love can become the foundation and central event of human life?

The need to answer these questions becomes all the more

63

serious when we see how unreal the experience of Christ is for so many people today. The need becomes all the more serious when we see that in fact few people, a relative minority in the Catholic life of parishes, colleges, and even seminaries give evidence of any real "feel" for the transforming embrace of a Father's Love which becomes authentic and alive in the experience of Christ.' People may have an idea of that Love, an idea of that experience, perhaps an understanding of the idea — even enough to profess it, believe it, even to teach it in catechism or theology class. But there's a whole dimension of understanding missing. There is a weight, an understanding, an impact that isn't there because there is no deep experience of what is believed, in effect no deep experience of Christian Faith.

For comparison, let's use a parallel. We know and believe as true that we will feel great sadness, deep loss and separation when we lose someone we love. We can even achieve some measure of understanding of this idea without experiencing its truth. But actually, it is only in the face of a real experience that the weight, impact, and power of that truth emerge.

So it is in trying to understand the experience of Christian Faith — that I am called at the heart of Christianity to become one with Christ in the arms of His loving Father, knowing deeply in Him the experience of His Father's Love! This is, I suppose, an idea of Christian Faith we can all understand and even believe to some degree without experiencing it as real, but as long as it remains purely an idea, there is still something about it that must remain to some extent vague and ambiguous. It still doesn't make "sense," and I have no handle on the idea without an experience of it. It is as if I were dangling from a cliff with nothing solid to hold onto and nothing solid upon which to fall. I need something more than words, ideas, abstractions and the analogies which they give us. I need something to see and touch, an experience worth more than thousands of words standing alone.

Can I attempt through words then an effort to render present an experience of God? Can I attempt through words an effort to go beyond what we do .when we paint a picture, or when we graphically illustrate an idea with examples and parallels? Can I attempt through words an effort to go beyond my analogies? I want to generate through .words that vision and dimension of understanding that comes only from an experience, when we see and touch — whether it be water, death, fire, food, or in this case, the Person of Jesus and His Love. But as in the case of all of these realities, are words enough? Can we come to the point where we experience the Presence of God through words?

I for one cannot say that my words lead to a *full* and mature idea of what Christian Faith is in its essential core and substance, nor can my words lead to the critical significance of Faith for men today unless they can in fact render present an experience of Jesus. Unless my words communicate not only ideas, but an experience of Christ as well, any idea of Faith I may come up with falls short and remains hollow. It stands incomplete and loses its full weight; I have denied it its rightful impact and power.

I am focusing here on a very central and pivotal issue. What can I do with only words and writing if I'm *saying* that any full or "mature" idea of Christian Faith has to be as well an experience of God. Unless this is the case, whatever idea of Faith we have is truncated, incomplete, not whole. It is the tragedy and distortion of a Faith that does not lead to Food, that does not lead to Christ.' It is ultimately a Faith which will fail to move us. A central, pivotal issue for me is whether my words and writing can lead to Food, to an experience of God, and not simply to more ideas about Christ, not simply to deeper insight and reflection, not simply to gospel values and biblical ideas.

There are many with me who have no problem understanding the central point that I'm driving at here and my emphasis on it. Behind it there may be a conviction that Christian Churches of today are much too cerebral and often purely intellectual. What is needed today is not more ideas about Christ, but an experience of Him. To settle for more ideas about Christ is as ludicrous as settling for only ideas about food. Settling for ideas about food is not at all adequate because the need of man is for so much more than just an idea of food. Food has to be as well an experience we consume and devour. And yet in no less a real way and even more essentially, Jesus Christ is the Food of man that has to be for us so much more than simply an idea.

Now what do I think I can accomplish with all my writing if I can give no more than words and the ideas they convey to us? With all my metaphors, comparisons, and parallels, I need to accomplish something more than just a transmission of ideas and concepts about Jesus. What good is my whole enterprise if through all my effort I could only tell you what Food is like or what Light is like? Our need is for real Food, for real Light. Yet only true Bread can give us this experience of real Food and the full, "mature" understanding that can come only with this experience. Only real Light will help us to see, and as well to understand the Light for what it really is. What then can I do with only words and writing if my goal is to give real Food and true Light? An idea of Faith "come of age," developed to maturity and full stature has to involve this dimension of real experience.' Christian Faith must lead to real Food, to real Light. It is like experiencing dawn for the first time — a sense of living in a whole new world or sphere of existence. Yet, can words render present a whole new world? Can they communicate an experience of God?

With the proclamation of the Gospel, I think they can.·

Chapter 3

God Gave Them A Living Word

"...he received living words to give to us..."
Acts 7:38
"...the gospel ...is the power of salvation..."
- Romans 1:16
"...Faith comes through hearing, and hearing...
through preaching about Christ..."
-Romans 10:17

Can my words go beyond ideas and render present the full vision and experience of Christian Faith? In a sense, can my words render present a whole new world? Can they give a Food' and Light beyond what the world can give or see or know? Can my words communicate an experience of God?

I think they can. I say this and believe this because I am a Christian, and a Christian can proclaim the gospel that is Jesus. But even to speak this "Good News" is to speak a "living word." This is a word when spoken that is God's power; it is divine Presence and transforming Love for any man ready to hear it and receive it. It is a word in which God lives and through which He Himself touches us. It is a living Word born two thousand years ago, but even before that, reaching out to our world from God since the dawn of man.

To explain this "living word" further, it is sufficient to say that I describe a word issuing forth from the heart of a John Paul II or a Mother Teresa; I describe a word issuing forth from the heart of any man that is in any real measure one with the Heart of God, with Jesus Himself' — so much so, it is no longer we who live, but Christ Who lives in us.;

That Christians can speak such a word is a fact that is foreign or forgotten by many within the Church today, and yet it is nevertheless a fact that is true and awesome in its potential ramifications.

God Wants To Intervene Decisively in Our Lives

Why do I say this? The fact of a "living word" tells us first of all that it was never the intention of God to leave us only with an idea of His Love, but much more radically it is clearly His intention to intervene in our lives with an *experience* of His Love, with an experience of His Spirit. An idea of His Love would not be enough for man any more than an idea of food, or father, or friend would be enough without an experience of the same. Yet it is clearly the intention of God *through "living words"* to provide man with more than an idea, with precisely an experience of His Love as well.

The implications of all this are that a book on Christian Faith, even this book, does not need to stop short of an experience of Christ. No more or less than the event of Mass or the effort of prayer, the presentation of Christian Faith should not stop short and does not need to stop short of an experience of Christ. Without this experience we strip the Mass, prayer, and the presentation of Christian Faith of its heart and foundation. Like the Mass or prayer, Christian Faith should rest and build upon an experience of God's power, as a house is built upon a foundation or as a man thrives upon his heart as a source of life. Without this experience of God we are left with the tragedy of ritual and words which talk about God as if "Christmas" never happened, and even more tragically as if "Christmas" doesn't happen every day - and I mean "Christmas" as the reality of Christ being born into our world and penetrating into our lives as an experience of a real Person,; not simply as an idea or a new philosophy.

And yet this is precisely the tragedy that looms behind so much of what is written and said in the Christian Churches of our time. The books, the homilies, the efforts of religious education offer us a shallow and empty Christian Faith which leaves us purely and solely on the level of ideas without any experience of God's power or Person.'

How does this come across, or what could I point out that might help someone share what I see? I think it is a simple question of examining the lack of efficacy or transforming effect in much of what is said and written in Christianity today. For instance with "Christian" books circulating prolifically in Churches today, an immediate experience with many of them is that they lack something. While they may be harmless, they are in fact also useless as a source of Life or as an experience of God. To read them is like sitting down for a meal and finding only an empty plate or a glass that is never filled. This is to say that their words do nothing to release a Power that can change our lives, or nothing to communicate a Presence that can change the world, or even more difficult, a Presence that can transform the heart of man. After their words fill the air, the blind do not see, the deaf do not hear, the lame do not walk, the dead are not raised to Life, and the poor and rich as well are still empty of joys Their words are not a word of power; they are not a word of God. This is not to say that I don't find these books insightful, filled with challenging and even provocative ideas, but it is to say that they don't go far enough. They could and should also be a "word of God," a "living word."

It should in fact be a charism and privilege characteristic of the Christian that he can write and speak this "living word." or "word of God." Though the New Testament writings contain no word of God spoken after the second century, it was never the intention and desire of the Father to cease speaking a word of power to the heart of men. It was never His intention to no longer touch the hearts of men with a word that would move them, drive them, and transform them irresistibly with divine Love. It was never the intention or desire of the Father that Christians of all centuries not be a people of prophets, a people releasing and speaking a word that by its "very nature releases power to achieve its vision and dream. It was never His intention and desire that Christians not be prophets letting precisely this kind of word issue forth from their heart to light a sick world with the healing and transforming Fire of a Father's Love.

This book is my attempt to speak this kind of word. It is my effort to speak a word of God to the men and women of my own day and age. At the same time, it is nothing more than my effort to do precisely what Christians should be able to do as something within their proper rights, prerogative, and power. In approach, this book is filled with stories of healing, some which pertaining to me are difficult to share, yet really at the heart of this book's design is an effort to speak "living words.'" "living words" that will communicate and release for men to touch and see, an experience of God's transforming Love.

Whether or not I am in fact doing this is not within my role or purpose to say. But if a certain sense of hunger deep within the heart ceases to exist, if people begin to see God more deeply, perhaps even for the first time, if chains fall from the hands of the powerless and the poor,' if strength to cope reaches out to the weakness of Peter sinking in a storm at sea, if the force of Life draws near and death begins to lose its oppressive stings — if any of these moments occur, I would venture to say that in some real way, my words have touched a word of God. If there is this experience of transforming' Presence, I would venture to say that I am communicating not only stories of healing, but also a guide to God's Love and power. I would venture to say that I have then effectively communicated a word of God, a "living Word."

Chapter 4

A "Living Word"
As A "Secret Weapon"

The "Living Word" and the Christian's power to speak it, is really our secret weapon with which to attack the problems of our time. This is the second reason why our God-given right to speak a word living with God's Presence has enormous and awesome ramifications for the Church and society at this point in the history of the Western world. Basically, Christianity has a secret weapon with which to change Western society and the whole world as well. It is a weapon that Christian Churches probe for and drastically need, yet the irony of this whole situation is that they have the weapon within their grasp already.

By what reason can it be stated that a "living word"[1] is really a secret weapon that can change the world? The ground of the argument rests on the fact that when a "word" communicates or releases the Presence of Jesus into our world, we have rendered present a creative energy, a transforming Force, a Spirit, a power that by the fact of its being present among us *has to* change the world[2] - the world, that is, in a scriptural sense where love is crippled and lame, and where life can be boring, desolate, and empty of joy.[3] This world once touched by Christ can no longer be merely the "world" of scripture, the place that is divorced, severed and cut off from God, a place devoid of His Presence and dynamic Love, a kingdom stripped and robbed of its King.

Like a radioactive element then, a living word releases divine

71

Presence into our world and that Presence is needed drastically as much as man needs food, as much as he needs a heart to be the vital foundation for the continuance of life.

Why in fact do I say "needed," and why do I underscore the need to be of such magnitude? What leads me to do so is the evidence and fact of such need that I see before me, and that each of us must weigh for ourselves. Groping, floundering, searching, hungering and thirsting are seen in the world today,' and more tragically, even in Catholicism today and the witness of other Christian Churches. How are Christians unique or in stark contrast to the world, when for all their belief in Jesus as the Food,² comfort, Light and transforming Love of men, they are simply people who stand with the worlds in not seeing Him, knowing Him, or experiencing His Love?

For this compelling reason alone, the men of today, even those espousing belief in Jesus, need an ancient word spoken long ago which like the Mass is both Light· and Power — a Light that leads, instructs, and guides them, but also a healing experience of God present in power, an experience of God that they can touch and see.° The men of today need a "a word" *which not only leads, but lives as well.* They need a living word that guides them to the point where they can understand how to make contact with the living God.

They need a word that gives not only an idea of God, but a word that leads of its very nature to an experience of His Love as well, and as I speak of His Love I am speaking of the Love that is His Holy Spirit. The men of today, even those espousing belief in Jesus, show evidence of great need for a living word, or stated another way, for a sacramental word that can effect a real contact with God precisely because it renders in itself an experience of transforming Love, an experience of Christ's Spirit that one can know and feel. They need a word from the Father's heart,· a Word Who leads us to, and provides in Himself, an experience of transforming' Power that can drastically alter our present experience of the world. It is an experience of transforming Power which can not only change radically our understanding of the world by raising it from its death to Love, but an experiences which alone provides the key and clue of what Christianity is all about, of what Catholicism and all Christianity involves at its own

72

heart and core as an essential imperative.

Now I can only ask that one feel and observe with me the questioning and searching of the world and Church of our own time, and examine whether the hunger and need surrounding us does not in fact call out precisely for this ancient word that is itself not only guidance and light, but also power; a word that leads and instructs, but that in itself is also living and active with God's Presence.

Where if anywhere is the impact, power and critical experience of that transforming Love to which Faith should lead?' Why is there floundering, groping, searching, hungering, thirsting? Why does the rich man of America still say in the face of so much affluence, "... What do I still lack?", It is because today, as always, men need proclaimed and spoken a special word born two thousand years ago, but even before that reaching out to our world from God since the dawn of man., Men today as always need this special word that is more than a dogmatic assertion, a theological statement, an idea or concept, more than a word spoken, proclaimed, and taught in our classes that merely leads, instructs, guides and lights the way. We need further a word spoken and proclaimed that provides power, a word that releases in itself an experience of Christ, an experience in our own day of the "good news" of God present to us in power as transforming Love beyond all reason. Until men hear this kind of word that not only instructs and guides, but provides in itself an experience of God's Love, the world and even the Church remain unmoved in the face of Faith definitions and theological assertions.

Yet it is precisely men who are unmoved, searching, and hungry that are seen everywhere today. In the face of all the words taught, proclaimed, and heard, a multitude of people everywhere are falling short of any experience of God's Love. There is clearly a hunger for a word spoken and proclaimed, that will unlock an experience of contact with the power and Love of the Father. There is a hunger for a word spoken and proclaimed, that will unleash an experience of Jesus' Spirit longing to embrace them., Until this word is spoken, it will be heard again and again: "How do I' know there is a God?" "Where is God — why doesn't He come down?" "What is it to experience the Father's Love?" "What on earth is the specific, objective experience of Christ that I refer to as if it

73

were real?"

These are questions that are really asked and that surface in the searching and hungering of the present-day world and even the present-day Church. In a real sense they articulate this hunger. They do this, just as the cries of the newborn child* warn us of his hunger even before food has ever touched his lips, even before the child really knows what it is for which he cries. The "crying out" is a sign. So too these questions are a sign and warning that resound throughout the world and Christianity of our own day. They signal a "crying out" for "Food." A "crying out" for precisely the experience of Christ which alone can heal the searching and hunger all-pervasive in the world and Churches of our own time.

And so a "living word" must be spoken, and it is a thrilling fact to know that the Christian can speak it.' For though the hungering of man for Christ cries out on every side, there is the awareness as well, that the Christian has within his grasp *the word,* "the secret weapon," that can release within our lives precisely this experience of God for which the world yearns.

An image for this world today, in its hunger and emptiness, can be expressed so effectively in the experience of John Wesley on his first transatlantic cruise. It was here that he experienced Christians in prayer, deeply at peace, during an austere and formidable storm. He longed to enter into this peace. Yet he was left dangling and uncertain not knowing how to enter into this strength and peace. There was a real question for him just as there is for scores of others today. The question for him might be put in any one of the following ways: How do I come into what you people have? Don't leave me with just metaphors and ideas. I want to experience God. I want His Spirit surging into my existence. I want to feel "picked up and embraced" by the Father of Christ! Now show me the way to this feeling experience. How do I become overshadowed with the Power Who is the Spirit of the Risen Jesus?[3]

Or perhaps the questions should be phrased differently, yet in a way that it would be most critical to hear them: Can you speak a "living word"? Can your words communicate an experience of

*A reference here to an analogy used in the *Antioch Weekend Manual,* where it appears as an example in the "Church in the World" talk.

God? Can they give not only guidance and instruction, but Food and strength beyond what the world can give or see or know? Can your words render present a whole new world filled and transformed with the creative Love of God, just as a wave swells the sea' or as Love transforms the heart of stone?²

And it is a thrilling and exalting fact to me to know that the Christian can speak precisely this kind of word, a word, a secret weapon, drastically needed to heal the hunger of a dark world starving for God as never before.

PART IV

For all who believe,
questions that are crucial
toward the contemplation of God.

Chapter 1

Does Your Faith Broaden Your Horizon To Include The Reality And Experience of God...?

Does your Faith broaden your horizon to include the reality and experience of God,' God present in power as transforming Lover

When I was a little boy of about seven years, I remember with so many vivid and touching memories the endless hours of play in the field near the river behind my home. But there is one afternoon I spent here which I shall never forget all the days of my life on earth. A "little gang" of us were playing "hide and seek" and I was waiting a long time for someone to come and find me.

Finally with some sense of frustration, I moved cautiously back to the field from my hiding place in Jimmie's back yard. When I got there I found my little friends assembled together, and gazing off into a brilliant afternoon sky. Their attention was wholly fixed on something, and they had wholly forgotten about me. I remember that I began to run. I wanted to join them, for I was filled with a sense of fascination and wonderment about whatever the cause might be for such a bizarre intrusion halting the fun of a lazy summer day.

As I approached and started yelling for some attention, one of the little girls in the group drew back and pointed out for me what was going on. I remember her being so excited as I would be too in a few minutes. Her face was glowing with the excitement of a secret too good to keep to herself. "Jesus and Mary are in the sky," she said. "Jesus and Mary are in the clouds!"

I ran to where all of the gang stood, looking and gazing as if there were nothing else in the world of any worth to see. I looked up with them and joined them in a vision of Jesus and Mary that thrilled my heart with joy beyond belief, beyond what one could imagine or ask for.'

There in the afternoon sky, set against the brillance of a summer sun, we clearly saw a dark but very sharp silhouette of Jesus and Mary speaking to each other in a part between the clouds. The clouds veiled from view everything beneath their shoulders. But in the movement of their faces we could clearly tell that they were talking.

Now I don't know how long all this lasted and I don't even care. Perhaps the others would be able to say. I remember who they are and know where each of them is even today. In any case they would definitely be able to confirm the story that I tell.

What I do care about however, is why I should feel at all any need or compulsion to seek compelling proof and witness that this tale of my transforming vision is in fact true. People will often ask me to defend myself, even people who are Christians that claim to have "great Faith." "How do you know you were not imagining all that?" they will say. Others will ask, "But how can you be sure it was something of God?"

And all I can do in defense is bear witness to what I have seen and heard.² What my heart was able to "see" and "hear" and experience on that day was the embrace and transforming power of a Father's Love reaching out to touch us in His Word made flesh.³ How do I know? The key and crux identifying the Father's Love and establishing the real experience of God as nothing less than this is always *the effect, the change, the power of transformation* in our own heart.* This is how we always know that what we see or hear and experience in our hearts is something of God — whereas before I was blind, now I see; whereas before I was dead, now I am alive,' raised to a Life and freedom born in the embrace of a

*See the *Life* of St Teresa of Avila, P. 234, the *Autobiography of St. Teresa of Avila,* Doubleday & Co., Garden City, New York, 1960

Father's Love.'

I know once again, even more deeply, the transforming joy and freedom that I once knew so clearly on a day long ago in the experience of running with my father. I was free of all care and fear in the overwhelming experience of his love embracing me. It is the freedom and joy of the Son, or for that matter of the Brides — the freedom and joy known to Christ and born in the embrace of a Father's Love, a Love that transforms, heals, and raises to Life.

That is all I can say in defense of my story, a defense that I never really want to make at all. I have often gone back to that field in my thoughts, in my memories, and in my dreams, and just the reminiscence of that event touches my heart and human spirit once again with transforming Presence. This transforming effect on my heart and human spirit continues even to this moment. And this continuing effect more than anything else compels and intensifies my conviction even to this moment, that what I saw that summer day long ago was truly of God.

Am I crazy? Eccentric? A singular Christian standing necessarily apart from a multitude of believers who would never dare to boast of visions and dreams coming from a world or realm beyond our own?' It would seem to me that if only because Christian Faith builds and founds itself on an *experience* of God's Power, I, with all Christians, should be compelled and am in fact compelled to defend my *experience* of the supernatural — Jesus, the Life of God revealed to me and in rne.'° In fact, I stand with all authentic believers in being driven and compelled with the urgency of Paul" to defend and bear witness to what I have seen and heard of the experience of God's power" that is the vital heart and foundation of my Christian Faith. This experience of power should be the foundation of Christian Faith,' without which my Faith proves hollow and barren, a Faith building on sand."

This is at the core and basis of my discomfort when my story of long ago meets with interrogation and cross-examination and oppressive scrutiny. Why in fact should I ever have to feel any need and compulsion to give cogent and compelling demonstration or defense for an experience like this among believers? The nature of this experience is in substance nothing more or less than the experience of God's transforming Love and Presence that is the one foundation on which the Christian Faith of all believers is supposed to stand. Faith should rest on an experience of God's power effective and present in our experience.

And this is why I always climax the defense of my story and its authenticity with a question: Why does your Faith not lead you to an experience of God present in power as transforming Love? Or put another way: Why does your Faith not broaden your horizon to include the powerful reality and transforming experience of the Holy Spirit?' It disturbs me that so many ideas of Christian Faith today in fact do not do this. Yet the Faith which leads to Christian Life, to Christ's Life in us, is itself an experience of grace and power. Any Presence of the Love of Jesus issuing forth into the world through my life, words, deeds, and work is precisely an experience beyond my own power unaided by grace. It is precisely an experience beyond my power unaided by an intimate, transforming union with the Spirit of the Father.

For this experience we need only embrace an authentic idea of Christian Faith that will open us to the fact and reality that just beyond the horizon the Light of a divine world is there ready to rise upon our darkness and insufficiency. We need only embrace an authentic idea of Christian Faith that will lead us to "leap" into the arms of a loving Father, Who longs to be alive and real to our experience. We need only embrace a true Faith which will lift our eyes to see that Love Who pours forth His Presence day to day beyond all I can ask or imagine possible. We need only embrace a true Faith that will open our ears to hear that Voice Who calls out to us"...through all the earth...and...to the end of the world. '

But so many ideas of Faith do not cause men to lift their eyes and see — whether it be lifting our eyes to behold visions from a world beyond, or simply lifting our eyes from the sand to behold His Presence in the sea, perhaps the penetration of His Presence in the panorama of an ocean bay playing with the brilliant sky of an evening sun. So many ideas of Faith circulate today that do not allow us to see visions of His Love all around us or dream things a world without God could never know.'⁰

They are spurious ideas of Faith that join the folly of hell in its futile effort "to swallow the sea" or block the sun from the earth.* Yes, an idea of Faith that would preclude, deny, or even ignore an

* An allusion here to the thought of Bishop Fulton Sheen, given during an open retreat in the Diocese of Gary, Ind., Sept. 10-13, 1973.

experience of God present in power to the believer as Love that transforms and heals and raises to Life, is a "Faith" consumed with folly. It is a "Faith" trying to hide the rising sun that would pierce the darkness and its fear. It is a "Faith" that would block a tidal wave of Love from streaming and surging forth into the existence and experience of men. It is an idea of Faith that is a wolf in sheep's clothing.' It is unbelief disguised as Faith. It is in reality the cynicism and the unbelief of a dark world drowning in its isolation and distance from the Light and Fire of a Father's Love.

For the fact is that even today, in this hour, a Father's Love reaching out incessantly to embrace the heart of believing melt' is an all-pervasive reality as real and critical as the air we breathe. The fact is that even today a Father's Love moving the lives of men and transforming them irresistibly is an all-prevasive Force as present in our world as life itself. It is a Love as undeniable, critical, and indispensable as the sun shining in the strength of noon-day.

And more and more people today are lifting their eyes to see this Love. More and more people today know a divine compulsion within the depths of their hearts, a compulsion to leap into the arms of an all-loving Father Who has become alive and real to their experience in the Person of Christ's Spirit. The story of one priest in particular captures so well this reawakening to the reality of God's Love reverberating and resonating throughout Christianity today.

He witnesses that he suffered emptiness even for many years of his ministry, knowing only a "Faith" that left him impoverished and without Bread.[6] But so many things began to happen — words, counsels, coincidence, invitations, happenings and events strangely at the right time and in the right place — and suddenly you might say there was a divine compulsion within him to lift his eyes from the sand and behold the sea. He began to know a Christian Faith where God's Word would move his heart irresistibly.' It would move and heal and feed. At the deepest level of his heart there was now satisfaction and fulfillment[8] where before hunger and thirst had been an endless plague; all of life had been an endless quest, a search for Food[9] and strength° the world could not give."

But now the invitation, the appeal, the sustaining nourishment of Living Bread' had made itself felt with power.' There was nowhere else to go; there was nothing else to do but respond to Love present in power. Driven irresistibly or perhaps drawn irresistibly,' the priest began to seek "the healing Light"* and transforming Fire of a Father's Love. Real Presence had called him to look beyond his darkness' toward Light ready to rise upon his existence for the price of his openness to intimacy, embrace, and transforming union.' He opened himself to the reality of 'a Father Who longs to be present in power and real to our experience as Love that transforms and heals.

He had only to believe, to lift his eyes and open his heart. He had only "to leap" into the arms of a loving Father, and all life became the experience of Presence and Power intimately with him, burning' the heart.' Before, prayer, the Mass, the Scripture, the anointing with holy oil — all had been ritual, form without power,' words reaching out to a reality beyond what he could know or feel or see.' Now, each was an event placing God within this grasp" and releasing to his heart an experience of God's transforming and healing Love.

Now he can share of the divine Force moving through him," moving him to"...signs too deep for words...";" moving him to know power beyond all he could ask, imagine, or express." In the moments of anointing the sick with the holy oil, he has known an overwhelming sense of Presence rushing through his hands to touch the lame and infirm with healing Fire." He has even shared from the pulpit in the homilies of Sunday morning Mass his experience of God present in power as Love that will transform and heal, if only we will "leap" into the arms of God our Father. As he speaks of the power he has seen and heard," many people have been shocked to attention, hearing, or better stated, "heeding"'' for the first time a Word that caused them to lift their eyes from the sand and behold the sea.

And though I speak of one specific priest, he is one of a multitude," one among many of whom I could share the same. He is one of so many priests, religious, and a multitude of the "faithful" for whom baptism, prayer, and Eucharist are no longer rituals devoid of power," but each

---

*An allusion here to the title of an excellent book by Agnes Sanford, dealing with the theme of this chapter.

event touch our lives with transforming Love. They are events that truly "baptize," "fill," immerse," and "transform" with the Spirit of Jesus,' not only in word or name, but in substance and fact.²

Chapter 2

At The Summit Of Christian Experience

"Are You Dying Young?"

My thoughts turn to a story that tries to explain the meaning of the question, "Are You Dying Young?"[1] It was directed to me by a dear friend at a funeral during my last year at Holy Cross.* My friend asked the question during a magnificent eulogy fOr his younger brother. His brother had died a few days before in an automobile accident on the eve of graduating from high school.

Are you dying young? A story that best explains to me the meaning of this question took place centuries ago. I first "saw" the story in a movie** when I was a little boy. All the people in my neighborhood including myself loved it and believed it, and never questioned its truth.

For when I was a child, a Faith moved freely among the people of our city and country that never questioned the reality of God present in power' among us. And it was never a bizarre and preposterous experience when a story proclaiming this same fact surged forward into our existence from a distant and ancient past. We believed as fact without a second thought that God had become man, that the Incarnation had actually happened; that Jesus, a man like ourselves, had risen from the dead; that to this day He was a Real Presence still among us, even in His Body and Blood at Holy Mass.'

---

*This close friend is John Moriarty, who graduated with me from the College of the Holy Cross in May, '68.
**The movie I allude to here is the"Miracle of Marcellino." Like so many movies and books of its kind however, it has disappeared from contemporary society.

I don't know whether the story actually happened. But I believe and my Faith tells me — that every day the Reality of a Father's Love does in fact touch lives[2] exactly as the story described — with power that heals,[3] raises to life,[4] and transforms' with j oy.[6]

I would also say that if the story actually happened, it didn't happen the way I tell it. I have made the story my own, and it has become a unique reflection of the vision and Faith and experience of my own heart. You might say when I first received the story, that it was like any small, living child. But the story has now become my child — over the years it has grown and developed and come to maturity under my care and direction. You might even say that it has come to bear my likeness. It has become my story and the story of the Christian — the story of any man called to die young. Put another way, it is the story of what it means to move and strive each day toward one goal' before all others — the ever- deepening experience of Jesus as the Father's Love.'

I can only promise that as the story has grown with the passing of years, I have taken extreme care to protect its gift for speaking the Truth.[9] I can only promise that the story I tell still speaks the Truth, as I'm sure it did from the very first time it was told.

The story begins hundreds of years ago with the father and mother of an infant boy leaving him in a basket at the doors of a Dominican friary in Spain. The friars at the monastery find the child, and receive him into their love and care.'''

The child was named Marcellino, and as he grew and became a healthy young boy, well into the age where reason and decision are possible, he became a crafty little guy, full of tricks, and wiles, and mischief. Though the monks had always welcomed him into every area of their life, they now had a further reason to keep him near and within watching distance — and therefore out of trouble.

He ate with them and helped them in the fields as much as a little boy could. But most important for our story, he became a regular assistant in the kitchen for the "big fat friar" in charge of clean-up after every meal. It really wasn't that bad a job. The friar was a jolly man, a kind of "Friar Tuck," who talked and *sang* endlessly as they worked. Now this of course could have made the job unbearable, but the fact is the friar would feed Marcellino, and himself, with all kinds of "little goodies" as they "inched away" at the task at hand.

However, there was one restriction placed on Marcellino, and I never really knew why, except perhaps that I think it was a part of this grand design to keep the boy under a watchful eye, aware of his every move. Marcellino was told not to enter the room at the top of a stairwell near the kitchen. It was a closed room leading to the attic of the abbey. He was not even to open the door or go up the stairs. That whole area was to be restricted for him, beyond his reach and a mystery which he was not to touch. He was not to know or experience what was in this room.

I'm not going to explain the meaning of this story. It should be clear enough to speak for itself. However, we do need "a key" at times to unlock the meaning of words which might otherwise not speak to us. Let me then only provide a "key," and say that in the Christianity of our own day there is a door and room very much like this room. There are as well many men who bear the name and wear the garb of a Father's Love, and yet they place the door and room beyond our grasp.' They tell us that we cannot know or experience what is in that room. It is to be and always has been, they say, wholly shrouded in mystery, like a Templet veiled from our view and vision, beyond what we can touch and see.

But each time Marcellino would walk by the stairs he would look up at the door, and his heart was drawn as if by some unseen but nevertheless real and irresistible Force. He waited for his moment, for a way to escape the ever-watchful eye and scrutiny of his kitchen guardian. And when that moment would come, he would follow the desire of his heart.

The moment came, or I should say it was always there, but it only suddenly dawned on him. It occured to him one afternoon after helping in the kitchen, that at this precise moment each day he had the perfect opportunity to go up the stairs without ever meeting any resistance.

The clue to understanding this came with the realization that there was one missing link in the "grande design" of the friars to monitor his every move. After lunch all the friars moved out into the fields once again or back to their rooms — all but one — the "big fat friar." He stayed with Marcellino in the kitchen, and talked and sang endlessly. Now it had been very much growing in Marcellino's awareness that this "big fat friar" who talked and sang endlessly, could in fact talk and sing for quite some length of time caring little whether Marcellino, or anyone else for that matter, was really there to respond.

Marcellino would test his insight for a few days, for he knew that if this opportunity was available, he would have found the "missing link," the flaw in the "grande design." He would have found an opening, a chance, a moment, when he could quietly move up the stairs unnoticed. And as he suspected his insight bore true beyond a doubt. When asked questions, he would not answer; when remarks could elicit a response, none was given. Marcellino could drift quietly and totally out of the monk's sight, world, and awareness because he never seemed to even be there to begin with. And drift out of the "fat friar's" sight is exactly what Marcellino did. However, through it all the words of the monk continued to flow forth in an endless stream. The little boy crept carefully out of the kitchen to the stairs nearby, and looking all around for his final check of a way made smooth and clear,' he moved upward and forward. His heart was drawn yet pounding in the face of mystery, and still it all seemed so easy! Marcellino's final fear was an unbearable thought that the door might be locked or the entrance barred, chained, and closed forever.

But it wasn't, for in fact no one can lock that door or close that room to any man. Though heavy with a huge iron latch, the door gave way easily for Marcellino. He peeked inside carefully, only to see something he had never seen before, something of which he had never before been told.'

It was a crucifix, which to Marcellino appeared larger than life. It had a figure of Jesus upon it as huge as any man Marcellino had ever seen. He had never seen Jesus like this before — as a Fact, a Person, Something as big and as real to his experience as life itself. He was filled with fear! He closed the door quickly and tightly, and ran down the stairs. This entire first encounter lasted only a few seconds. However, none of this frightful reaction of our little friend should really surprise us because truthfully, when we first encounter Jesus there is some sense of fear and apprehension, as there always is in the face of something new, strange, or foreign to anything we have ever known or touched. This is true even if it is something good and exciting; but especially if it is Something larger than anything we can conceive or understand or imagine.'

However, notice that I say "first encounter." I say it because that sense of being irresistibly drawn did not stop. Marcellino had in a sense "touched" Something and seen Something[2] that moved him and drew his heart back to that room with an appeal and attraction unlike anything else, as nothing else and no other desire could affect him or absorb him.

It was only two days later that Marcellino decided to sneak away and up the stairway once again, and again with not even a threat of resistance from the kitchen friar. But this time he would bring bread, thinking that perhaps Jesus was hungry.

You see, Marcellino was still at an age where he was one among many children who cannot conceive of Jesus as only a lifeless statue, but only as Someone very real. There is perhaps a time before children "see"[3] Jesus, and experience Him as clearly as Marcellino, but they never doubt His reality. They have a Faith that He is there, that they are talking with Someone real,[4] and that inevitably a moment will come when they will clearly behold and experience the Presence of His transforming Love[5] and Power.[6] Perhaps there could be a "strange twist" to this story, if we could speak as well of a Father Who can only feel irresistibly drawn to bring Bread to his lifeless and suffering children' — and Who can feel so drawn only with Love beyond all we can ask or understand.[8] Yet we would be left with a paradox. The "strange twist" that would speak of a Father's Love bringing Bread[9] to His Children strikes in fact at the heart and core of the story's meaning.

At any rate something of this Love was very present in Marcellino and moving his heart to bring bread to the crucified Lord. He climbed the stairs unnoticed and opened the door. He boldly but slowly walked inside, and for the first time the fear began to dissolve. He could not feel fear for very long in the Presence of Love.[10]

Marcellino moved further and further away from the door toward the crucifix, and the Figure upon it. When near enough to touch the nail through Jesus' feet, he held the bread up to the face of Jesus with his right hand.

Only a moment passed, the gaze of the boy fixed upon the Lord, and the gaze of Love fixed upon the boy." The left hand of the Lord began to move. It reached slowly to receive what was given and offered by a little boy whose love and attention were lost to all other care.' Was there brilliant Light as Jesus came down from His cross to sit with the child and take him into His arms and embrace? I know that wherever Jesus is, there is intense Light'... There was in fact present for Marcellino the transforming Light of a Father's Love that would take away forever the darkness and "night"[3] deep within the heart of an orphan* from birth.

What happened from here? I remember the film moving on to show the scene many times repeated — the scene of Jesus holding the child in the room beyond limits and shrouded in mystery. And Marcellino continued to wait anxiously every day, for the moment when he would sneak away and up the stairs. That moment became the focus[2] of his day. You might say he began to "die young". He began to plan and move and strive each day toward one goal before all others — this ever-deepening experience of Jesus.

Marcellino was never caught. It couldn't be any other way. Each time Marcellino would bring bread, and each time Jesus would break the Bread' and share it with him.

As they ate, Jesus would speak of the Love of His Father. And Marcellino found that as they ate together, his heart would burn with a sense of this Father's Love present and alive in the Person of Jesus.' Marcellino found too that not only the Person of Jesus, but His every Word, every Word that issued forth from within Him, was alive and effusive with the Presence of this Father's Love.' As Marcellino quickly climbed to the room each day, he began to feel more and more that in running toward the experience of Jesus, he was running toward the Father's Love, toward God Himself. Marcellilno had come in fact to embrace Jesus as God.[2] When he would leap into His arms, he was living, moving, having his being in the embrace of a Father's Love." There was for Marcellino in that embrace, a Life," a Power, a freedom," a healing, and a joy which the world could never givelsand which his heart could never leave.

With each day's visit Marcellino found it harder and harder to leave Jesus. It was only because he lingered on so long one day, that the kitchen friar finally noticed that Marcellino was not with him. He wandered out of

89

the kitchen only to glance around, but stood amazed as he saw a strange Light streaming forth from the room beyond limits at the top of the stairs. And as fast as his fat legs would carry him, the big kitchen friar "ran" up the stairs to see.

I thank God for that day, because had no one ever seen what transpired between Jesus and the boy, we would never know the story of Marcellino. I say this because that was the last day that Marcellino spent upon the earth and in our world.

The kitchen friar on that important day could only dare to peek in, but he heard Jesus speak of His Father. He saw Marcellino and Jesus eating together and Jesus holding the boy close to His heart.' However above all, he heard the conversation which teaches me of Truth¹ — the most vital truth that Faith needs to teach.

He heard the boy say to the Lord, "I wish I had a Father and Mother that loved me like your Father." And Jesus looking at the boy said, "You do. My Father is your Father.' My Mother is your Mother."' Then Jesus asked Marcellino if he would want to be with them, and oblivious to all other care he answered, "Oh, yes! Yes! Yes...

This was too much for the "big, fat" friar. He wanted all the brothers to see, and yet he could not leave his vision. He only turned for a moment and yelled downstairs, "Come and see.' Come and see. Jesus is here." The screaming produced a flurry throughout the little Spanish abbey, and all of the brothers ran up the stairs to where Jesus held the boy who was "dying young." They arrived just in time to confirm the truth of the big friar's story. They watched the boy disappear, going to the Father in the embrace of Jesus.'

That boy is me. That boy is the disciple whom Jesus loves.' It is the boy who was "dying young." It is the boy who wanted before all else to move ever more deeply through Jesus into the experience of theFather's Love. It is the boy who wanted Bread; the boy who wanted Christianity; the boy who wanted the experience of God present in power as Love that transforms, heals, raises to Life and joy. It is the boy who wanted this experience of Faith and this experience to which Christian Faith must lead before all else.' And "...when the Son of Man comes again..." may He find this Faith flourishing upon the earth, in abundance as the sand on the shore of the sea or as the stars in the sky.'º

Chapter 3

Toward A Conclusion -
The Nerve Center of Faith

True Faith Leads to the Experience of God

True Faith will always lead to the Spirit of God's Love as real and present and transforming,' for without Him, Faith becomes hollow, deficient, only a shell and sham remaining of its rightful substance. Why do I say this? I say it because Faith calls out for this experience of His Love as much as the body cries out for each of its parts, or as the part of the body cries out for the whole for its own completion. Faith cries out for this experience of God as the hand cries out for the head and the heart, knowing it is lifeless without them, or as the dead body cries out for soul and spirit for the same reason.

Unless Faith includes this experience of God present in power as Christ's Spirit, as Love that transforms and heals, Faith is incomplete, sterile, robbed of its Life and power. Faith "lacks something"; and becomes hungry; so also the people confessing it and seeking it for Life in God. They are seeking it for what it cannot give, and their journey will lead to a dead-end. Embracing this empty Faith, this plastic Faith that is hungry, sterile, and complaining, such people join the chorus of pagan men today, in so many ways crying out for the experience of God to complete them and make them whole.

These people of lifeless Faith, though well-intentioned, suffer the same plight as pagan men, for their "Faith" still leaves them without God,' without the experience of His Love alive, present, and embracing us in the Person of Christ's Spirit. Hunger is hunger, and in fact the hunger of their empty Faith is no different from the rampant hunger of so many godless men today. Theirs is the same hunger which in a thousand ways still cries out for God much as physical hunger cries out for bread, much as roots cry out for food, even as fire reaches out desperately to the fact of fuel, or light to the sustaining source of its power.

People of lifeless Faith, of empty Faith, betray with this same hunger that their "Faith" has not helped them. It is Faith without the experience of God, Faith without its heart, goal, and essential life-giving substance. For in all this, the experience of God is a Foods all-critical to the vital core and purpose of Faith as much as God is a Food all-critical to the healing and freedom of man. In fact, Christian Faith has as its central task to bring this Food to men, and with this Food that is the fact and experience of God, to heal them and set them free.

Excitement Of Faith That Leads To God

It is this essential character of true Faith as an entering into the Life and experience of God in the Spirit of Christ, which explains the excitment I attach to Faith seen in all the fullness and richness of itsmeaning. Faith should intrinsically lead us to the experience of God, to the Bread that is critically needed for man's Life, strength, and survival in Love. Christian Faith then becomes the excitment of finding Food in the midst of famine, of finding God in the midst of a hunger for Him among contemporary men, that grows more acute and insatiable with the passing of days and weeks and years.

This experience of God as "Food" describes the experience to which Faith leads, an experience that is crucially so much more than just an image or metaphor. I cannot effectively express in words how Faith seen as the decision to enter divine Love is really a decision to find real "Bread in the wilderness."" It is really a decision to experience the trauma of healing and freedom generated in the embrace of God's power.'

There is something vast, sweeping, and cosmic about this

*This is an allusion to a title of a book written by Thomas Merton.

experience of Faith. It has all the excitement and thrill of a Columbus discovering America. Imagine the discovery that a whole new world lies before us waiting for us to explore and enjoy.jAnd as Galileo led us to the fact of new worlds, as Copernicus led us to transform our vision of all creation, it is as well precisely the task of Faith to transform in the Light and experience of God, our vision of Life, our world, and of all creation.¹ How can Christian Faith do less than this when it confronts us with this critical Food, when it confronts us with this experience of God present in power as Love that transforms and heals and lifts us out of fear into freedom?

This then is the experience of Christian Faith. It cannot be seen as anything less than a decision to enter union with divine Love, and in that union to know God as a real experience, an experience as real as water, fire, electricity, or the air we breathe. All this is accomplished in Jesus. Faith is the experience and the excitement of entering into the Life of Jesus, and knowing in His Spirit the healing, vitality, strength, and freedom born in the embrace of a Father's Love. This is the heart and substance of Christian Faith. The experience of Christian Faith has as its core and live nerve, this sense of knowing in union with Jesus the experience of God.³ That is the experience which is a Food all-critical to men. That is the experience of critical importance to the Life, healing and freedom of the Christian and all men as well.

It is even crucial to any belief in, or sustained hope for the sanctity of human existence, the dignity of man, or the achievement of all Christian ideals, for these will only be realized and come into being as the fruit' of this deeper focus — this pursuit of Christian Faith as an entering into the Life of Jesus and knowing in Him the embrace of a Father's Love as real and present and transforming. Do I appear to go too far? What then is the body without a soul, man without a heart, all these moral values and even human life itself without the Love that is God, without the Love that is ours only in Christ?' A focus then on the pursuit of Christian Faith seen in all the fullness and richness of its meaning is pivotal. Without this fullness, the "good news" of Christianity is really never proclaimed and men never really see and experience all that God wants to give.'

To Proclaim Faith That Leads Us In Christ To The Experience of God

What inspires the effort of my writing is then precisely a desire to prevent this tragedy by presenting Faith in all of its fullnes, excitment, and power. What inspires my effort is a desire to present Faith seen as all that it is and nothing less, as the critical Food that is God, leading men to Life, strength, healing, and freedom.

In doing this, I write in particular for the multitude of Christian "Faithful" whose only response to the fact of real Food in the experience of Jesus is a thunderous silence and indifference. There might even be a cursory assent and approval to the idea of being a Christian, but what still portrays to me a critical problem in the way they understand their Christian Faith is the simple fact that for all their belief they remain hungry, groping, searching, thirsty.' True Faith would lead them to the experience of Christ, to real Food Who takes away hunger, to Living Water Who can cast the experience of thirst to a land of distant memory.²

I write then for all men, but mainly for this multitude, so that the Christian Faith which so many of them understand as something purely conceptual, cerebral, and abstract, might now move and expand beyond an idea in the region of mind to an experience in the realm of the heart as well. I write that Jesus as Bread for my Life might not become just a "Faith-proposition" to which I assent, but a Person to Whom I can attest and to Whom I can bear witness as present and real to my experience.⁴ My assent to the fact that I am a Temple and Sanctuary of God's Presence,⁵ that I am an earthen vessel bearing transcendent powers must not merely become a "tenet of Faith" to which I assent with my lips, but a fact of which my heart can feel and speak, an experience my eyes can see and my hands can touch.'

I write that in a tangible world of flesh and blood my eyes might behold the new dawn of an ancient dream⁷ — God becoming man once more, God once more walking the earth in the lives of Christian people imbued to overflowing with the real experience of His Love.⁹ I write that once more "Echoes of an Ancient Word," might resound through the city of our own day, and reach out with all the force of God for roots in the earth of our own time.¹⁰

Scripture Citations

Pg.

Scripture Citations

Scripture Citations

Pg.	No. Citation		Pg.	No. Citation
40	1	Mt. 14:28-31	42	7 Jn. 16:9-11
40	1	Lk. 24:13-32	42	8 Phil. 3:20-21
40	1	Jn. 11:32-36	42	8 2 Cor. 3:17-18
40	1	Hos. 141-4	42	8 Gal. 5:1, 13-25
40	1	Is. 40:11	42	8 Rom. 8:9-11
40	1	Col. 1:28-29	42	9 Acts 1:5
40	1	2 Cor. 5:13-15	42	9 Rom. 6:3-11
40	2	Roin. 6:3-11	42	9 Jn. 1:33
40	2	Phil. 3:7-14	42	9 Acts 19:1-6
40	3	Lk. 24:13-32	42	10 Rom. 8:31-39, esp. 37
41	1	Jn. 17:20-26	42	10 Mt. 14:30-31
41	1	Jn. 5:19-20	42	10 Heb. 2:14-15
41	1	Acts 17:28	42	10 1 Jn. 5:3-5
41	1	Mt. 14:28-31	42	10 Jn. 16:32-33
41	1	Jn. 6:57	42	10 Col. 1:15-20
41	1	Hos. 2:19-20 cf. Jn. 3:28-30; 17:3	42	10 1 Cor. 15:22-28
		cf. Mt. 9:15; 11:27 Rev. 21:2-3	42	10 Mt. 16:18
41	2	Jn. 8:12	42	10 Rev. 19:11-16
41	2	Jn. 12:35-36	42	10 Eph. 1:17-23
41	2	1 Jn. 1:5, 8	42	10 1 Jn. 1:5
41	3	Acts 2:17	42	10 Jn. 10:27-30
41	3	Joel 2:28	42	10 Lk. 10:17-20
41	3	Mt. 11:2-5	42	10 Lk. 5:17
41	4	Jn. 11:40	42	10 Lk. 6:19
41	4	Jn. 3:36; 5:24; 17:3	42	10 Lk. 8:46
41	4	Mt. 14:28-31	42	11 Mt. 15:8
41	4	Lk. 24:13-32, esp. 30-32	42	12 Acts 2:17
41	4	Eph. 1:19	42	12 Joel 2:28
41	5	Jn. 14:17	42	12 Mt. 11:2-5
42	1	Phil. 4:7	42	13 Phil. 3:7-14
42	1	Jn. 16:21-22	42	13 Rom. 8:35-39
42	1	Jn. 14:27	42	13 Eph. 3:16-19
42	1	Jn. 16:32-33	42	13 Gal. 2:19-20
42	2	Ps. 36-7-9	42	13 Jn. 17:20-26
42	2	Ps. 42:1-2	42	14 Jn. 6:68
42	2	Ps. 63:1-8	42	15 Lk. 9:33
42	2	Ps. 16, 46, 91	42	15 Mt. 17:4
42	2	Acts 17:27-28	43	1 Jn. 17:20-26
42	3	Gal. 5:22	43	1 Jn. 3:28-29; 17:3
42	3	Eph. 2:14	43	1 cf. Hosea 2:19-20
42	4	Ps. 16	43	1 Jn. 5:19-20
42	4	Ps. 23; Mt. 5:8	43	1 Acts 17:28
42	4	Ps. 73:23-25	43	1 Jn. 6:57; Jn. 15:4-5; Jn. 10:30
42	5	Gal. 5:24	43	2 Col. 1:28-29
42	5	Rom. 8:1-11	43	2 2 Cor. 5:13-15
42	6	Ps. 73:26	43	2 2 Cor. 4:7-11
42	6	Ps. 16:8; Acts 3:16	43	3 Rom. 8:14-17
42	6	Phil. 4:13	43	3 Jn. 11:39-40
42	6	Ps. 59:17	43	3 Mt. 14:28-31
42	7	Ps. 16:11	43	3 Lk. 24:13-32
42	7	Gal. 5:22	43	3 Jn. 11:32-36

Scripture Citations

Scripture Citations

Pg.	No. Citation		Pg.	No. Citation
54	13 Heb. 12:1-5; 2:5-3:6		53	13 Mt. 14:30-31
54	14 1 Tim. 2:3-4, 5-6		53	13 Gal. 5:1
54	14 Jn. 6:37		53	13 Heb. 2:14-15
56	1 Jn. 1:12, 14, 16-18		54	1 Jn. 12:27
56	1 1 Jn. 4:13-16		54	2 Jn. 17:20-26
56	1 Jn. 5:19-20		54	2 Jn. 5:19-20
56	1 Jn. 5:24-26		54	2 Acts 17-28
56	1 Mt. 11:27		54	2 Mt. 14:28-31
56	1 Acts 17:27-28		54	2 Jn. 6:57 Also: Hos. 2:19-20, cf.
56	1 Jn. 14:18-21, 23			Jn. 3:28-30; 17:3 cf. Mt. 9:15;
56	2 Jn. 1:12			11:27-30 Rev. 21:2-3
56	2 2 Tim. 3:5		54	3 Phil. 4:7
56	2 Rev. 3:1-2		54	3 Jn. 14:27
56	2 Rev. 2:4		54	3 Jn. 16:32-33
56	3 Lk. 3:4		54	4 Jn. 16:32-33
56	4 Jn. 8:12		54	4 Mt. 14:19-31
56	4 Lk. 12:35-36		54	4 Jn. 12:31-32; Jn. 19:30, 34
56	5 Lk. 12:49		54	4 Lk. 24:13-32, esp. 30
56	6 Jn. 1:12-14, 16-18		54	5 2 Cor. 4:7
56	6 1 Jn. 4:13-16		54	6 Acts 2:17
56	6 Jn. 5:19-20, 24-26		54	7 1 Jn. 4:17-18
56	6 Mt. 11:27-30		54	7 Heb. 2:14-15
56	6 Acts 17:27-28		54	7 Rom. 8:9-11
56	6 Jn. 14:18-21, 23		54	7 Phil. 3:20-21
56	6 Rom. 8:1-4, 13-19, 21-23, 29		54	7 2 Cor. 3:17-18
56	6 Heb. 12:1-5, 2:5-3:6		54	7 Gal. 5:1, 13-25
56	6 Jn. 17:20-26		54	8 Eph. 3:20
57	1 Jn. 17:20-26		54	8 1 Cor. 2:9-10
57	1 Jn. 5:39-40		54	9 2 Cor. 6:10
57	1 Jn. 6:40		54	10 1 Jn. 4:16
57	1 Jn. 14:7; 10:10; 17:3		54	11 Jn. 14:17
57	1 Mt. 11:27		54	12 1 Cor. 7:31
57	2 Phil 3:7-14		54	12 1 Jn. 1:5-6
57	3 Rom. 8:35-39		54	12 2 Cor. 3:16-18
57	3 Eph. 3:16		54	12 2 Cor. 4:3-4, 6
57	3 Gal. 2:19-20		54	12 2 Cor. 5:16-17
57	4 Jn. 10:25-29		54	12 1 Jn. 3:2
57	4 Jn. 5:18-27		54	12 2 Cor. 4:18
57	4 1 Jn. 4:12-16		54	12 Rev. 21:1-7
57	4 Jn. 16:32-33		54	13 Eph. 1:5
57	4 Jn. 14:18-23		54	13 Gal. 2:20
57	4 Jn. 14:5-11		54	13 2 Cor. 13:5-6
57	4 Lk. 10:21-22		54	13 Acts 3:16; 19:2
57	4 Jn. 3:35-36		54	13 1 Jn. 1:1-4
57	4 Jn. 17:20-26		54	13 Jn. 17:20-26
57	4 Jn. 1:1, 14-16, 18		54	13 Jn. 5:19-20, 24-26, 39-40
57	5 1 Jn. 1:1-4		54	13 Jn. 6:40
57	5 Jn. 17:20-26		54	13 Jn. 14:6; 10:10; 17:3
57	5 Jn. 1:12-14; 16-18		54	13 • Mt. 11:27-30
57	5 Acts 1:8		54	13 Jn. 14:18-23
57	5 1 Cor. 2:2-5		54	13 Rom. 8:1-11, 13-19, 21-23, 29

Scripture Citations

Scripture Citations

Pg.	No. Citation	Pg.	No. Citation
78	11 James 4:4	79	16 Jn. 10:26
79	1 Jn. 6:51	79	16 Rom. 1:5
79	2 Jn. 6:68-69	79	16 Rom. 16:26
79	2 Lk. 9:33	79	17 Acts 2:17
79	2 Mt. 17:4	79	18 2 Tim. 3:5
79	3 Jn. 6:44	79	18 Mt. 15:8
79	3 Jn. 12;32	79	18 Rev. 3:1
79	3 Col. 1:29	79	19 Acts 1:5
79	3 2 Cor. 5:14	79	19 Rom. 6:3-11
79	3 Gal. 4:19	79	19 Jn. 1:33
79	4 Lk. 24:25-32, esp. 30-31	79	19 Acts 19:1-6, esp. 2
79	5 Jn. 1:12	79	19 Acts 2:37-38
79	5 Jn. 3:46	80	1 1 Jn. 3:18
79	5 Jn. 10:26	81	1 1 Cor. 11:36; Rom. 6:3-11, esp. 10
79	5 Rom. 1:5	81	1 Jn. 12:31-32; Jn. 19:30, 34 cf.
79	5 Rom. 16:26		Mt. 14:29-31; Lk. 24:13-32, esp.
79	6 Lk. 24:32		30-31
79	7 Jn. 1:12	81	2 Eph. 3:14-20
79	7 Jn. 3:36	81	2 Rom. 8:9-11
79	7 Jn. 10:26	81	2 2 Tim. 1:11-14
79	7 Jn. 11:40	81	2 2 Cor. 3:17-18; Rom. 5:4-5
79	7 Jn. 11:36	81	2 2 Cor. 4:5-9
79	7 Rom. 1:5	81	2 2 Cor. 4:5-9
79	7 Rom. 16:26	81	2 1 Jn. 4:13-17
79	7 Mt. 14:28-31	81	3 Lk. 5:17
79	7 Lk. 24:25-32	81	3 Lk. 6:19
79	8 2 Tim. 3:5	81	3 Lk. 8:46
79	8 Mt. 15:8	81	3 Ps. 73:26
79	9 Jn. 14:17	81	3 Ps. 16:8
79	9 Eph. 3:20	81	3 Acts 3:16; 19:2
79	9 1 Cor. 2:9-10	81	3 Phil. 4:13
79	9 Phil. 4:7	81	3 Ps. 59:17
79	10 1 Cor. 11:26; Rom. 6:3-11, esp. 10	81	3 Rom. 8:31-39, esp. 37
79	10 Jn. 12:31-32; Jn. 19:39, 34	81	3 Mt. 14:30-31
79	10 Mt. 14:29-31; Lk. 24:13-32,	81	3 Heb. 2:14-15
	esp. 30-31	81	3 1 Jn. 5:305
79	10 Jn. 6:56; 6:51; 15:4-6, cf. Jn.	81	3 Jn. 16:32-33
	6:56; 1 Cor. 10:14-21	81	3 Col. 1:15-20
79	11 Lk. 5:17	81	3 1 Cor. 15:22-28
79	11 Lk. 6:19	81	3 Mt. 16:18
79	11 Lk. 8:46; Jn. 14:12; Acts 6:8	81	3 Rev. 19:11-16
79	11 Acts 5:12-16	81	3 Eph. 1:17-23
79	11 Acts 19:1-6, esp. 2	81	3 1 Jn. 1:5
79	11 Acts 2:37-38	81	3 Jn. 10:27-30
79	11 Acts 4:29-33	81	3 Lk. 10:17-20
79	12 Rom. 8:26	81	4 Jn. 1:14
79	13 Eph. 3:16-20	81	5 Lk. 24:4-7
79	14 Lk. 12:49	81	5 Mt. 28:5-10
79	15 Acts 4:19-20	81	5 Mk. 16:6-8
79.	16 Jn. 1:12	81	5 Jn. 20:9-18
79	16 Jn. 3:36	81	5 Rev. 1:17-18

Scripture Citations

Pg.	No.	Citation	Pg.	No.	Citation
82	1	Lk. 24:30-31	82	10	Is. 40:11
82	2	Jn. 14:17	82	10	Hos. 11:1-4
82	2	2 Tim. 1:82	82	10	Mt. 14:28-31; Lk. 24:25-32, esp.
82	2	2 Pt. 1:8			30; Jn. 13:34-35
82	2	Hos. 2:19-20	83	1	2 Tim. 3:5
82	2	Acts 3:16; 19:2-6	83	1	Rev. 3:1cf. Mt. 23:13-15
82	2	Eph. 1:5	83	2	Heb. 9:1-9, 24-26; 10:19-23
82	2	Gal. 2:20	83	3	Jn. 6:44
82	2	1 Jn. 1:1-4	83	3	Jn. 12:32
82	2	Jn. 17:20-26	83	3	Col. 1:29
82	2	Jn. 5:19-20, 24-26, 39-40	83	3	2 Cor. 5:14
82	2	Jn. 6:40	83	3	Gal. 4:19
82	2	Jn. 14:6; 10:10; 17:3	83	4	Ps. 37:4
82	2	Mt. 11:27-30; 9:15	83	4	Ps. 73:23-28•
82	2	Jn. 14:18-21, 23	84	1	Lk. 3:4-6
82	2	Rom. 8:1-11, 13-19, 21-23, 29	84	2	Mt. 11:27-30
82	2	Heb. 12:1-5, 2:5-3:6	84	3	Rom. 8:31, 35
82	3	Acts 3:4-10, 16	84	3	Jn. 6:35, 37, 40
82	3	Mt. 11:4-5	84	3	1 Tim. 2:4-6
82	3	Gal. 5:24	84	3	Jn. 27-29
82	3	Rom. 8:1-11	84	4	Lk. 10:23-24
82	4	Eph. 1:18-20	84	4	Mt. 13:16-17
82	4	Rom. 8:11	84	4	Eph. 3:16-20
82	4	Heb. 11:19	84	4	1 Cor. 2:9-10
82	4	Rom. 4:17	84	4	Jn. 14:17
82	5	Phil. 3:20-21	84	5	Eph. 3:14-20
82	5	2 Cor. 3:17-18	84	5	Rom. 8:19-11
82	5	Gal. 5:1, 13-25	84	5	2 Tim. 1:11-14
82	5	Rom. 8:9-11	84	5	2 Cor. 3:17-18; Rom. 5:4-5
82	6	Ps. 16:11	84	5	2 Cor. 4:5-9
82	6	Gal. 5:22	84	5	1 Jn. 4:13-17
82	6	Jn. 15:9-11	84	5	1 Jn. 1:1-4
82	6	Acts 3:4-10, 16	84	6	Mk. 10:32
82	6	Mt. 11:4-5	85	1	Eph. 3:17-20
82	7	Phil. 3:7-14	85	1	Phil. 4:7
82	7	Rom. 8:35-39	85	2	1 Jn. 1:1-4
82	7	Eph. 3:16-19	85	2	Jn. 1:18
82	7	Gal. 2:19-20	85	2	Jn. 17:25-26
82	8	Jn. 10:25-29	85	2	Jn. 14:17-21, 23
82	8	Jn. 5:19-27	85	3	Jn. 9:35-39, esp. 39
82	8	1 Jn. 4:12-16	85	4	Lk. 24:13-32
82	8	Jn. 16:32-33	85	5	Eph. 3:16-19
82	8	Jn. 14:18-23	85	5	Jn. 3:16
82	8	Jn. 14:6-11	85	5	Rom. 8:32
82	8	Lk. 10:21-22	85	5	Jn. 13:1; 19:30, 34
82	8	Jn. 3:35-36	85	5	Jn. 15:12-13; 19:30, 34
82	8	Jn. 17:20-26	85	5	Jn. 14:18-23
82	8	Jn. 1:1, 14-16, 18	85	6	1 Jn. 4:13-19
82	9	Jn. 14:6	85	6	Jn. 11:40
82	9	Jn. 17:17	85	6	Eph. 1:19
82	9	Jn. 8:31-32	85	7	Lk. 11:11-13

Scripture Citations

Pg. No. Citation

89	3 Jn. 6:27
89	3 Jn. 6:51
89	3 Jn. 6:53
89	4 Jn. 6:30-35
89	4 Is. 41:17-20
89	4 Ez. 37:1-14
89	5 Jn. 4:31-34
89	5 Jn. 6:35, 38, 51
89	5 Jn. 6:53-55
89	5 Jn. 6:57
89	5 Is. 55:1-3
89	6 Jn. 6:30-35
89	7 Jn. 5:19-21; Jn. 5:24-26
89	7 Acts 17:27-28
90	1 Rom.12:1-2
90	1 2 Cor. 5:15-18
90	2 Jn. 5:19-21
90	2 Jn. 5:24-26
90	2 Acts 17;27-28
90	2 Jn. 6:57
90	3 Jn. 1:12-14, 16-18
90	3 Jn. 10:10; 17:3
90	4 Jn. 15:5-8
90	4 Gal. 5:22
90	4 Mt. 6:33
90	5 Acts 2:17
90	5 Mt. 16:25-26
90	5 1 Cor. 13:1-3
90	5 1 Cor. 2:2-5
90	6 Mt. 19:20, 22
91	1 Mt. 19:20
91	2 Jn. 6:35
91	2 Jn. 4:13-15
91	3 Eph. 3:17-19
91	4 Jn. 14:17
91	4 2 Tim. 1:12
91	5 1 Cor. 3:16-17
91	6 2 Cor. 4:7
91	7 1 Jn. 1:1
91	8 Mt. 11:2-6
91	8 Rev. 21:2-5
91	9 Acts 2:17-18
91	10 Wis. 18:14

www.ingramcontent.com/pod-product-compliance
Lightning Source LLC
Chambersburg PA
CBHW032104080426
42733CB00006B/414